API Testing Recipes in Ruby

The problem solving guide to API Testing

Zhimin Zhan

API Testing Recipes in Ruby

The problem solving guide to API Testing

Zhimin Zhan

ISBN 978-1537344782

Also By Zhimin Zhan

Practical Web Test Automation

Watir Recipes

Selenium WebDriver Recipes in Ruby

Selenium WebDriver Recipes in Java

Learn Ruby Programming by Examples

Learn Swift Programming by Examples

Selenium WebDriver Recipes in Python

Selenium WebDriver Recipes in Node.js

Contents

CONTENTS

Preface

For the past 9 years, I have been providing test automation consultancy to software projects, mostly web-based applications. For testing web apps, I use Selenium WebDriver to drive browsers to perform functional testing. However, more often than not, I found myself testing some sorts of APIs such as SOAP or JSON web services. Different from many testers, I don't use GUI tool such as SoapUI, instead I use ruby scripts because it is more efficient, flexible, easier to integrate with CI servers, and more fun.

First, let me share with you a story. Once I joined a project to test a large number of XML over HTTP services. The test team used the tool set by the architect: JMeter, which is an open-source load testing tool. Soon I knew the reason for selecting JMeter. For security reasons, the XML services of the application are encrypted. JMeter can import the PCKS key file to do the encryption. However, there was a problem. To switch another key (as a different client), the tester needed to restart JMeter. So, I saw a group of poor testers typing in request XML and adding non-intuitive assertions in JMeter UI, frequently restarting JMeter to load another PCKS key. They were mostly doing manual testing using a load testing tool. I was assigned to perform similar tasks, but I did not want to do that way. I wrote a script to encrypt XML requests using different keys, invoking services and performing checks, all in easy-to-understand Ruby scripts. Furthermore, I got them all run in a Continuous integration (CI) server. In a few days, I managed to reduce a 3-week of the whole team's testing effort to a repeatable and fully automated test execution, under 20 minutes.

This explains my approach to API testing:

- fully automated, no manual intervention
- easy to run all test scripts (as regression testing), ideally in a CI server
- leverage easy to read and powerful Ruby script language

Traditionally, API are built for integration for enterprise software. Nowadays, API popularity skyrocketed with the rise in smartphone use, and most new software projects are developed for web and mobile platforms. Microservices architecture, developing a single application as a suite of small services exposed as HTTP resource API, is becoming a hot topic. This demands efficient API testing.

I classify API testing as one type of black-box testing does not involve driving UI. Testing restful web services returning JSON or XML certainly is API testing, So are test scripts to verify generated Excel, Zip and CSV. In my opinion, API testing can be used in conjunction with UI testing and benefit each other. For example,

- Submit a request in JSON format via WebService (API Testing)
- Drive the browser to complete a process (UI Testing)
- Download generated Excel report (UI Testing)
- Verify the Excel report (API Testing)
- Check the notification email (API testing or UI testing if used mailcatcher)

Who should read this book

This book is for testers or programmers who write (or want to learn) automated API tests. In order to get the most of this book, basic Ruby coding skill is required.

How to read this book

Usually, a 'recipe' book is a reference book. Readers can go directly to the part that interests them. For example, if you are not sure how to test DELETE Restful web services, you can look up in the Table of Contents, then go to the chapter 3.

Recipe test scripts

To help readers to learn more effectively, this book has a dedicated site[1] that contains the recipe test scripts and related resources.

As an old saying goes, "There's more than one way to skin a cat." You can achieve the same testing outcome with test scripts implemented in different ways. The recipe test scripts in this book are written for simplicity, and there is always room for improvement. But for many, to understand the solution quickly and get the job done are probably more important.

If you have a better and simpler way, please let me know.

---

[1]http://zhimin.com/books/api-testing-recipes-in-ruby

Send me feedback

I would appreciate your comments, suggestions, reports on errors in the book and the recipe test scripts. You may submit your feedback on the book's site.

Zhimin Zhan

Brisbane, Australia

1. Introduction

API (Application Programming Interface) is a collection of software operations that can be executed by other software applications, instead of human users. For example, an online store takes payment from a customer's credit card. The payment processing is typically done via API calls to a payment gateway such as PayPal. In this case, the payment gateway provides API, and the online store application is a consumer of API.

API testing is to verify the functionality of APIs.

API Testing vs Unit Testing

Unit testing is a type of white box testing performed by programmers at source code level (I prefer the term *Programmer Test* than *Unit Test*, as it is created and maintained by programmers). Unit Testing falls under white-box testing, API testing is largely under black-box testing.

> ### White-box testing vs Black-box testing
>
> In white-box testing, the tester is much more concerned with internal operations of the application. In black-box testing, the tester is only concerned with the functionality of the overall application, exercising only the inputs and checking the outputs.

API Testing vs GUI Testing

The main difference between GUI testing and API testing is obvious: we don't see the application's user interface in pure API testing. Besides, API testing differs UI Testing in:

- **Fast**

  API testing is usually an order of magnitude faster than a similar functional UI test. For example, to submit user registration form on a web page, a functional UI test case needs to open a browser, fill every field and click the 'Submit' button. If it is done by a web service API, just one single HTTP request with registration details typically in a XML or JSON.

- **More programming skills required**

  While good programming/scripting skills is required by API and functional UI testing (don't trust scriptless testing), people with no or little coding experience might still be able to get started with UI testing with the help of recorders. The nature of API testing, such as preparing test request data and parsing response data, requires more technical skills.

- **Less prone to changes**

  Comparing to GUI, changes to API is much less frequently. Even when an API-breaking change are unavoidable, providers will keep the current version (commonly renamed to `/api-v1/...`). However, developers usually won't have this kind of consideration when changing web pages.

Automated API Testing

Like functional testing, API testing can be done manually, and we see it is commonly done so. For example, to test a SOAP web service call, a test might perform the testing as below:

1. Open SoapUI tool
2. Create a new SOAP project and enter the initial WSDL (Web Services Description Language)
3. Select one service call and create a sample request
4. Edit the request XML
5. Invoke the web service
6. Verify the response returned

This is what I call manual API testing. Automated API testing is to invoke APIs by using automated test scripts. While we might use GUI tools to develop or debug test scripts, execution of test scripts (including verification) must be automated, no human intervention is required.

API testing substituted end-to-end functional testing

Ideally, full end-to-end functional testing via GUI is the best for ensuring software quality, if can be done successfully (*all functional UI tests executed many times a day with quick feedback*). However, few projects achieve this. Here is a text except from API Testing Wikipedia page[1]: "API testing is now considered critical for automating testing because APIs now serve as the primary interface to application logic and because GUI tests are difficult to maintain with the short release cycles and frequent changes commonly used with Agile software development and DevOps)." - Forrester 2015[2]

If you are interested in implementing end-to-end functional testing for web applications, read my other book Practical Web Test Automation[3].

An API test example

The test below invokes a web service to register a new user.

```
new_user_registration_xml  = <<END_OF_MESSAGE
<UserRegistration>
  <UserName>wisetester</UserName>
  <Email>testwisely01@gmail.com</Email>
  <Password>secret</Password>
</UserRegistration>
END_OF_MESSAGE

require 'httpclient'
http = HTTPClient.new
ws_url = "https://agileway.net/api/register"
resp = http.put(ws_url, new_user_registration_xml)
expect(resp.body).to include("Registration successful")
```

The above test posts a block of XML to register a new user. If it is done via UI, we need to follow many steps as this Selenium WebDriver test below:

---

[1]https://en.wikipedia.org/wiki/API_testing

[2]http://blogs.forrester.com/diego_lo_giudice/15-04-23-the_forrester_wave_evaluation_of_functional_test_automation_fta_is_out_and_its_all_about_going_be?cm_mmc=RSS-_-BT-_-63-_-blog_1769

[3]https://leanpub.com/practical-web-test-automation

```
driver = Selenium::WebDriver.for(:chrome)
driver.navigate.to("https://agileway.net")
driver.find_element(:link_text, "CREATE ACCOUNT").click
driver.find_element(:name, "email").send_keys("testwisely01@gmail.com")
driver.find_element(:name, "username").send_keys("wisetester")
driver.find_element(:name, "password").send_keys("secret")
driver.find_element(:name, "passwordConfirm").send_keys("secret")
driver.find_element(:xpath, "//input[@id='terms']/../i").click
driver.find_element(:id, "sign_up_btn").click
expect(driver.page_source).to include("Registration successful")
```

Skills required

Comparing to functional UI testing, writing API testing requires more technical skills. Without UI, we communicate with scripting.

- Knowledge of API and protocols

  Testers are required not only to know the top level protocol, but also the technologies or protocols underneath. For example, to write test scripts for SOAP web services, understanding HTTP, URL, XML and XPath is a must.
- Coding Skills

  Flexible API test scripts are in a syntax of programming language, such as Ruby and Python. To effectively develop and maintain test scripts, mastering programming concept and the language is a must. Having said that, the level required, at least at the beginning, for API testing is not as high as programmers.
- Parsing data data structures

  The messages (request and response) in API testing are commonly in XML and JSON format. Obviously, a good knowledge of them is a must. For example, parsing XML document using an XML processor and extract a specific element using XPath.

Use Ruby

API testing requires programming knowledge. Ruby is a dynamic, open source scripting language with a focus on simplicity and productivity, which make it ideal for writing test scripts. The below are three books on testing with Ruby from one publisher:

- "Scripted GUI Testing with Ruby"[4]
- "Everyday Scripting with Ruby: For Teams, Testers, and You"[5]
- "Continuous Testing with Ruby, Rails, and JavaScript"[6]

You might have heard of some popular testing frameworks in Ruby, such as:

- Watir - Web Application Testing in Ruby[7]
- Cucumber[8]
- Capybara[9]

The use of Ruby in test scripts does not mean we can only test services written in Ruby, not at all. In last 5 years, I have written API automated tests (all in Ruby) for APIs coded in Java and C#. The word API means an agreed standard. Take RESTful web services as an example, requests are sent to server by URL, responses are in XML or JSON format. It does not matter which language was used to implement the API.

 ## Ruby - Most valuable programming language

Based on this Quartz report[10], Ruby is also "the most valuable programming skills to have on a resume".

Install Ruby

- Windows: Ruby Installer for Windows[11]
- Mac OS X: Ruby 2.0 is included.
- Linux: can be easily installed, typically runs one command using a package manager

Add to your PATH.

---

[4]https://pragprog.com/book/idgtr/scripted-gui-testing-with-ruby

[5]https://pragprog.com/book/bmsft/everyday-scripting-with-ruby

[6]https://pragprog.com/book/rcctr/continuous-testing

[7]http://watir.com/

[8]https://cucumber.io/

[9]http://jnicklas.github.io/capybara/

[10]http://qz.com/298635/these-programming-languages-will-earn-you-the-most-money/

[11]http://rubyinstaller.org/

Install Gem

Ruby gems (a cool name for libraries in Ruby) are centrally hosted at rubygems.org[12]. To install or update a ruby gem, you need to be connected to Internet.

```
> gem install mail
```

The above command (run from a command line window) will download and install latest mail gem. The command below lists all the gems installed on your machine.

```
> gem list
```

RSpec Test Framework

To make the effective use of scripts for testing, we need to put them in a test framework that defines test structures and provides assertions (performing checks in test scripts). Typical choices are:

- xUnit Unit Test Frameworks such as JUnit (for Java), NUnit (for C#) and minitest (for Ruby).
- Behaviour Driven Frameworks such as RSpec and Cucumber (for Ruby).

In this book, I use RSpec, the de facto Behaviour Driven Development (BDD) framework for Ruby. Here is an example.

```ruby
describe "REST WebService" do

  it "REST - List all records" do
    http = HTTPClient.new
    resp = http.get("http://www.thomas-bayer.com/sqlrest/CUSTOMER")
    xml_doc = REXML::Document.new(resp.body)
    expect(xml_doc.root.elements.size).to be > 10
  end
```

---

[12]https://rubygems.org

```
it "REST - Get a record" do
  http = HTTPClient.new
  resp = http.get("http://www.thomas-bayer.com/sqlrest/CUSTOMER/4")
  expect(resp.body).to include("<CITY>Dallas</CITY>")
end

end
```

The keywords `describe` and `it` define the structure of a test script.

- **describe "..." do**

  Description of a collection of related test cases
- **it "..." do**

  Individual test case.

`expect().to` statements are called rspec-expectations, which are used to perform checks (also known as assertions).

You will find more about RSpec from its home page[13]. However, I honestly don't think it is necessary. The part used for test scripts is not much and quite intuitive. After studying and trying out some examples, you will be quite comfortable with RSpec.

Execution of RSpec tests is covered in Chapter 11.

Avoid SoapUI alike tools

This might send a shock for some readers, for them, SoapUI might be equivalent to API testing. In my opinion, working on test scripts in plain text directly is more flexible and simpler, which are important factors for test maintenance. Some will say, SoapUI does have scripting capability as well, using Groovy, a dynamic scripting language for the Java platform. Yes, that is true, but not good enough.

As we know, the real challenge of test automation (functional UI and API Testing) is not about writing the test, it is the maintenance of **all** regression tests. Please note the word "all", I highlight it here to show a perspective of API testing. If the maintenance of test scripts is hard, hiding the test scripts with a GUI layer is not a good approach. Instead, work on the test scripts directly to make them flexible by using programming techniques. Most software are written in this way, we certainly can do with the test scripts.

---

[13]http://rspec.info

The Win of plain text scripting for Selenium WebDriver

Nowadays, Selenium WebDriver undisputedly dominates functional testing for web applications. It was not the case 6 years ago. At that time, I found myself quite lonely at software testing conferences promoting open-source test scripting frameworks such as Watir and Selenium, surrounded by talks on fancy and expensive scriptless testing tools. Now many commercial functional testing tool vendors (including SmartBear, the new owner of SoapUI) have changed to support Selenium WebDriver. Bear in mind that all these commercial tools have some of own proprietary scripting as well under their GUI tool. Those script syntax were all lost to Selenium WebDriver for functional testing web apps. The main reasons of the success of Selenium WebDriver, in my opinion, are:

- text based
- empowered by programming
- good support by browser vendors

Comparing to Selenium WebDriver UI testing, developing test scripts for API testing is more like programming.

Developing plain text scripts does not mean typing them in NotePad. Like programmers, we do it in Integrated Development Environment (IDE, such as TestWise) or code editors (such as Sublime Text). This does not mean excluding helps from other GUI tools either. In fact, in next chapter, I will show you how to use free SoapUI open source edition to generate SOAP request templates.

The benefits of text scripting

The classic "The Pragmatic Programmer, From Journeyman to Master" book dedicated one chapter on "The Power of Text". If you haven't read it, I strongly recommend you to do so.

- **Integrate with other tests**

  For example, we can test a SOAP web service call, then go to the target web site to verify the content on a web page using Selenium WebDriver, all in one test case.
- **Easy to run**

  By using a build tool of a chosen scripting language, we can easily customize test executions, such as a suite of selected tests or test files in a pattern.

- **Flexible**

  Ruby is a powerful script language, and there are many libraries (called Gems) we can use. For example, for test scripts in RSpec, we can set certain test steps to run before and after each test case. For assertion, if we want to verify an element's value returned in SOAP is today's date, it is going to be quite difficult in SoapUI. In Ruby, it can be as simple as `expect(elem.text).to eq(today)`.

- **Script reuse**

  Ruby is a full-featured object oriented programming language. By using inheritance and modules, we can maximum the script reuse for much more maintainable test scripts.

- **Integrate with Continuous Integration**

  If we use a standard scripting (and open) language, it will be easier to integrate with CI servers. We can trigger an execution of all API tests with a click of button and get test report including historical results of each individual test. We can even distribute tests to multiple build machines to run them in parallel to greatly reduce the execution time.

Testing Tool

For API testing, the most involved tool is IDE or coding editor.

- Syntax highlight and validation
- Efficient Ruby code editing
- Flexible test execution and debugging

The tools Ruby programmers and testers use generally fall in the two categories as below:

Integrated Development Environment (IDE)

- Apatana[14], free
- NetBeans 6.9[15], free
- RubyMine[16], commercial

---

[14]http://www.aptana.com
[15]https://netbeans.org/downloads/6.9.1
[16]https://www.jetbrains.com/ruby/

Code Editor

- Atom[17], free
- TextMate[18], commercial, Mac only
- Sublime Text[19], commercial
- Visual Studio Code[20], free
- Vim[21], free

As you can see, there are many choices here. I use TestWise 5[22] (disclaimer: I created TestWise. The Pro edition is a commercial software). TestWise is a testing IDE that supports Selenium-WebDriver for testing web applications. I usually develop API tests and UI tests in one project, quite often, they benefit each other.

Run test in TestWise

To run all test cases in a test script file.

---

[17]https://atom.io/
[18]https://macromates.com/
[19]http://www.sublimetext.com/
[20]https://code.visualstudio.com/
[21]http://www.vim.org/
[22]http://testwisely.com/testwise

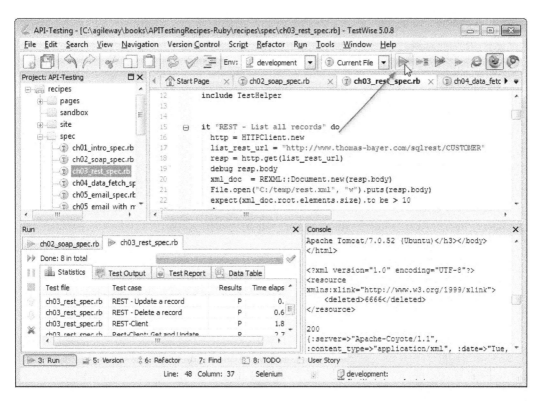

During developing (or debugging) tests, we just want to run a specific test case more commonly.

```
it "SOAP with dynamic request data" do
  http = Net::HTTP.new('www.w3schools.com', 80)
  template_erb_str = File.read( File.join(File.dirname(__FILE__), "..'
  @degree = 30
  request_xml =
  resp, data =
  {
    "SOAPActi
    "Content-
```

Run "SOAP with dynamic request data"	Ctrl+Shift+F10
Run test cases in 'ch02_soap_spec.rb'	Shift+F10
Run Selected Scripts Against Current Browser	Alt+F11
Run to this line	Alt+F10

Install new gems in TestWise 5

Select menu Tools -> "Show Ruby Gems"

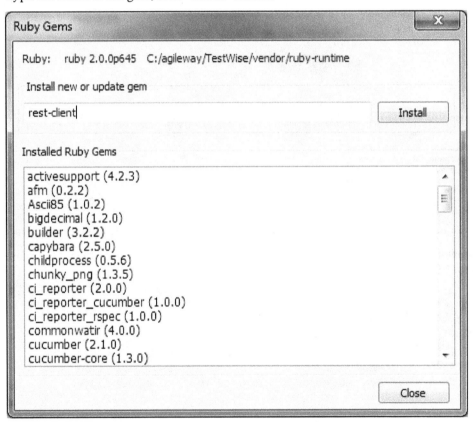

Type the name of the gem, click "Install" button.

2. SOAP Web Service

SOAP (Simple Object Access Protocol) is a messaging protocol that allows exchanging structured information in XML between computer applications. SOAP is often associated with the term "Web Service". A web service differs from a web site in that a web service provides information consumable by software rather than humans.

Commonly, a programmer's approach is to use generated classes from Web Service Definition Language (WSDL) to make web services calls. The code (or test) is in a compiled language such as Java or C#, calling the generated proxy code via serialization and deserialization. If you get a bit confused, you are not alone. Some unpleasant memories came back to me when I wrote the previous sentence.

I am going to show a simple and back-to-basic way to test SOAP web services, an approach I have used successfully in a number of projects.

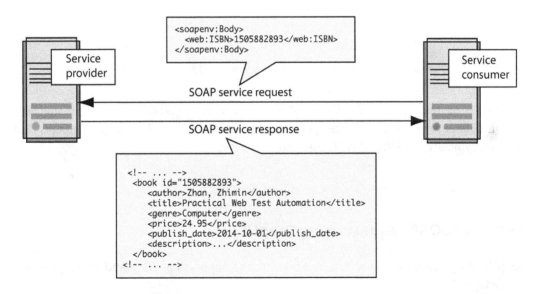

To test a SOAP web service, there are three steps:

1. Construct SOAP Request from WSDL

2. Post request to Web Service
3. Parse returned response XML to perform assertion

Construct SOAP Request

SOAP Web service is identified by its EndPoint, a URL. Here is an example: W3Schools'
temperature conversion service.

`http://www.w3schools.com/xml/tempconvert.asmx`

http://www.w3schools.com/xml/tempconvert.asmx?op=CelsiusToFahrenheit

But the one we really care is Web Service Definition Language (WSDL). As its name suggests,
WSDL defines web services. More specifically, it defines the XML request it accepts and
returns. Typically, the URL of WSDL is: EndPoint + ?WSDL.

`http://www.w3schools.com/xml/tempconvert.asmx?WSDL`

Generate SOAP request using SoapUI

SoapUI[1] is a popular open source web service testing application. The standard SoapUI (non
Pro) edition is free.

---

[1]http://smartbear.com/news/press-releases/smartbear-acquiring-web-services-testing-tool/

1. Create new SoapUI Project with WSDL

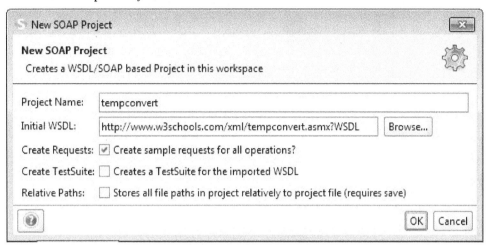

2. Select target operation and select 'Request 1' under it

Normally, the sample request generated from SoapUI is fine. In this particular case, the sample request for this w3school's web service is not right (the previous version was OK). The namespace prefix shall be 'x' instead of 'x\'. The actual string for the namespace prefix does not matter, the issue is with the '\' character. To fix it, just replace 'x\' to 'x'.

Previous version of Temperature Conversion Service The WSDL *http://www.w3schools.com/webservic* which was no longer available. The generated request in SoapUI was directly invokable.

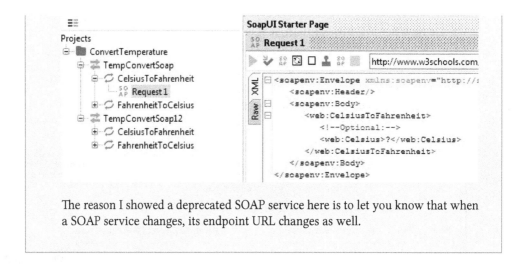

The reason I showed a deprecated SOAP service here is to let you know that when a SOAP service changes, its endpoint URL changes as well.

Copy the request XML to clipboard.

3. Test Web Service (optional)

   Feel free to change the request data (replacing '?') and invoke web service to see what response the web service will return.

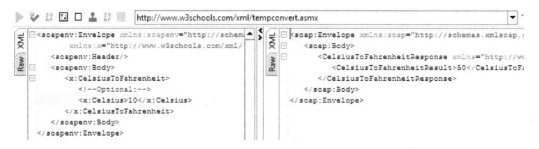

WSDL is a standard. There are many other tools that generate sample request XML. I simply use SoapUI as an example here.

SOAP Web Service call with Ruby

Based on the sample request XML generated from SoapUI,

```
request_xml = <<END_OF_MESSAGE
<?xml version="1.0" encoding="utf-8"?>
<soapenv:Envelope xmlns:soapenv="http://schemas.xmlsoap.org/soap/envelope/"
                  xmlns:x="http://www.w3schools.com/xml/">
  <soapenv:Header/>
  <soapenv:Body>
    <x:CelsiusToFahrenheit>
        <x:Celsius>10</x:Celsius>
    </x:CelsiusToFahrenheit>
  </soapenv:Body>
</soapenv:Envelope>
END_OF_MESSAGE

http = Net::HTTP.new('www.w3schools.com', 80)
resp, data = http.post("/xml/tempconvert.asmx", request_xml,
    {
        "SOAPAction" => "http://www.w3schools.com/xml/CelsiusToFahrenheit",
        "Content-Type" => "text/xml",
        "Host" => "www.w3schools.com",
    }
  )
```

As you can see from the above, the key data we need are:

- **Request XML**, filling values in the template generated from SoapUI
- **SOAPAction**, can be found in SoapUI, set in request headers
- **Webservice endpoint.**

Verify response body

After successful invocation of a SOAP Web service call, we get response. For API testing, it is usually a good idea to dump the response, `puts resp.body` writes to output or `File.open('dump.xml', 'w').write(resp.body)` saves to a file.

```
<?xml version="1.0" encoding="UTF-8"?>
<soap:Envelope xmlns:soap="http://schemas.xmlsoap.org/soap/envelope/" xmlns:\
xsd="http://www.w3.org/2001/XMLSchema" xmlns:xsi="http://www.w3.org/2001/XML\
Schema-instance">
  <soap:Body>
    <CelsiusToFahrenheitResponse xmlns="http://www.w3schools.com/xml/">
      <CelsiusToFahrenheitResult>50</CelsiusToFahrenheitResult>
    </CelsiusToFahrenheitResponse>
  </soap:Body>
</soap:Envelope>
```

Here are our simple assertions.

```
# ...

expect(resp.code).to eq("200") # OK
expect(resp.body).to include("<CelsiusToFahrenheitResult>50</CelsiusToFahren\
heitResult>")
```

Checking response code is to verify whether the call is OK. 200 is successful code for HTTP (SOAP is based on HTTP). The second assertion is to verify if a certain text is in the response body. I used "a string contains a sub-string" style assertion here. It is probably not kind of SOAP assertion you expected. You are right, we usually parse XML and verify data specifically. I will cover these techniques in later recipes. What I want to highlight here is that SOAP response is a string. Keep that in mind, you might find the use of string matching approaches such as regular expression.

Frankly, for this simple web service, I think the assertion is fine.

Verify response metadata

You may verify the response metadata, however, this mostly is not necessary. resp.each { |key, val| puts(key + ' = ' + val) } print out response metadata.

```
x-powered-by = ASP.NET
content-length = 408
x-aspnet-version = 4.0.30319
content-type = text/xml; charset=utf-8
date = Tue, 22 Dec 2015 00:00:38 GMT
server = Microsoft-IIS/7.5
connection = close
cache-control = private, max-age=0,public
```

SOAP Request with Dynamic Data

In the above SOAP test, the request data is hard coded: `<x:Celsius>10</x:Celsius>`. If we test with multiple sets of temperatures, we need to copy the request XML and make minor changes. This is not good, duplication is evil. One approach is to use templates:

1. Construct an template with the structure of request XML and placeholders for dynamic data
2. Generate message from a template with defined data

Construct request messages with templates

ERB (Embedded RuBy) is a built-in feature of Ruby for generating dynamic text from templates. A template is a text document that contains values marked with `<%= %>` that can be substituted. Here is a sample ERB template saved in file *c_to_f.xml.erb*.

```
<soapenv:Envelope xmlns:soapenv="http://schemas.xmlsoap.org/soap/envelope/"
                  xmlns:x="http://www.w3schools.com/xml/">
   <soapenv:Header/>
   <soapenv:Body>
      <x:CelsiusToFahrenheit>
         <x:Celsius><%= @degree %></x:Celsius>
      </x:CelsiusToFahrenheit>
   </soapenv:Body>
</soapenv:Envelope>
```

As you can see, the content of this template is very much like the request XML in the previous recipe, except that `<%= @degree %>` replaces the hard-coded template value.

ERB is part of the Ruby standard library, no installation is required, just use it.

Generate message from a template with defined data

```
template_erb_file = File.expand_path("../../testdata/c_to_f.xml.erb", __FILE\
__)
template_erb_str = File.read(template_erb_file)
@degree = 30              # changeable in your test script
erb = ERB.new(template_erb_str)
request_xml = erb.result(binding)
```

Line 1 and 2 are quite straightforward, reading content of a template file to a string. Line 3 defines an instance variable @degree with our test value.

The key statements here are erb = ERB.new(template_erb_str); erb.result(binding), which create an ERB template from a string and substitute

```
...
<x:Celsius><%= @degree %></x:Celsius>
...
```

with

```
...
<x:Celsius>30</x:Celsius>
...
```

Complete Test Script

```
require 'erb'
template_erb_file = File.expand_path("../../testdata/c_to_f.xml.erb", __FILE\
__)
template_erb_str = File.read(template_erb_file)
@degree = 30 # changeable in your test script
request_xml = ERB.new(template_erb_str).result(binding)

http = Net::HTTP.new('www.w3schools.com', 80)
resp, data = http.post("/xml/tempconvert.asmx", request_xml,
  {
```

```
    "SOAPAction" => "http://www.w3schools.com/xml/CelsiusToFahrenheit",
    "Content-Type" => "text/xml",
    "Host" => "www.w3schools.com",
  }
)
expect(resp.code).to eq("200") # OK
expect(resp.body).to include("<CelsiusToFahrenheitResult>86</CelsiusToFahren\
heitResult>")
```

Assert SOAP response

In previous test script, I just used the simple string contains check (`expect(resp.body).to include("<CelsiusToFahrenheitResult>86</CelsiusToFahrenheitResult>")`). This is OK but not preferred in general, as it is not specific.

Verifying SOAP response, in essence, is to parse a XML document and perform assertions. I will introduce a very common approach to XML parsing in Ruby here but will cover more in Chapter 4.

1. Parse XML using Nokogiri[2], a XML parser.
2. Strip out namespaces in XML document
3. Extract specific element using XPath to assert

Parsing XML

Here is a sample SOAP response message.

---

[2]http://www.nokogiri.org/

```
<?xml version="1.0" encoding="UTF-8"?>
<soap:Envelope xmlns:soap="http://schemas.xmlsoap.org/soap/envelope/" xmlns:\
xsd="http://www.w3.org/2001/XMLSchema" xmlns:xsi="http://www.w3.org/2001/XML\
Schema-instance">
  <soap:Body>
    <CelsiusToFahrenheitResponse xmlns="http://www.w3schools.com/webservices\
/">
      <CelsiusToFahrenheitResult>86</CelsiusToFahrenheitResult>
    </CelsiusToFahrenheitResponse>
  </soap:Body>
</soap:Envelope>
```

Parse it by using Nokogiri.

```
require 'nokogiri'  # gem install nokogiri
# resp.body is the above XML
xml_doc = Nokogiri.parse(resp.body)
```

Strip namespaces

The xmlns:soap and soap: are XML namespaces which are used to avoid element name conflicts. From a testing perspective, XML namespace have little value, and it makes locating specific elements using XPath harder. So remove them, here is how to use Nokogiri:

```
xml_doc.remove_namespaces!
puts xml_doc
```

The stripped XML without namespaces.

```
<?xml version="1.0" encoding="utf-8"?>
<Envelope>
  <Body>
    <CelsiusToFahrenheitResponse>
      <CelsiusToFahrenheitResult>86</CelsiusToFahrenheitResult>
    </CelsiusToFahrenheitResponse>
  </Body>
</Envelope>
```

Extract specific element with XPath

```
node = "//CelsiusToFahrenheitResponse/CelsiusToFahrenheitResult"
expect(xml_doc.xpath(node).text).to eq("86")
```

Use SOAP client: Savon

Savon[3] is a SOAP client for Ruby. Savon 'understands' WSDL (similar to SoapUI), invoking SOAP web service is more like a remote procedure call (RPC).

```
gem 'savon', '~> 2.0'
require 'savon'
client = Savon.client do
  wsdl "http://www.w3schools.com/xml/tempconvert.asmx?WSDL"
  convert_request_keys_to :camelcase   # change :foo_bar => FooBar
  open_timeout 20   # fail early when the service not available
  log true          # show in STDOUT
end
puts client.operations # => [:fahrenheit_to_celsius, :celsius_to_fahrenheit]
response = client.call(:celsius_to_fahrenheit) do
  message :celsius => "40"
end
puts response.to_s # get xml response string
puts response.body.inspect
fahrenheit = response.body[:celsius_to_fahrenheit_response][:celsius_to_fahr\
enheit_result]
expect(fahrenheit).to eq("104")
```

---

[3]https://github.com/savonrb/savon

Review

In this chapter, I showed testing SOAP web services with Ruby scripts:

1. Generate sample XML request (with help of SoapUI)
2. Construct ERB template
3. Generate request XML from ERB template with dynamic data
4. Invoke SOAP web service by POST request xml over HTTP (using HTTPClient)
5. Verify response data using XML processor (Nokogiri)

Some SoapUI users might ask what are the advantages of this ruby script approach over SoapUI? A lot, I listed some of them in Chapter 1 (under heading 'The benefits of text scripting'). Please read them if you haven't already. Try to compare these two approaches in the context of those benefits. Do not worry if some don't make much sense to you yet. I trust that you will understand more by working through the book.

3. RESTful Web Services

RESTful web services are based on Representational State Transfer (REST) architecture, commonly used for web based applications. Comparing to SOAP, RESTful web services are lightweight (less verbose message) and easier to implement for developers. It is easier to test, a good news to testers.

The four typical RESTful web services operations are: CRUD, an acronym for Create, Read, Update and Delete. The four basic functions of data records in database. CRUD operations, behind the scenes, invoke HTTP methods: PUT, GET, POST and DELETE respectively.

CRUD Operation	HTTP Method	Sample URL path
CREATE	PUT	/users
READ	GET	/users/12
UPDATE	POST	/users/12
DELETE	DELETE	/users/12

LIST all records

Listing all records is not one of CRUD operations. However it is commonly tested along with CRUD.

Sample Request

URL:	http://www.thomas-bayer.com/sqlrest/CUSTOMER
HTTP Method:	GET

Sample Response

```
<CUSTOMERList xmlns:xlink="http://www.w3.org/1999/xlink">
  <CUSTOMER xlink:href="http://www.thomas-bayer.com/sqlrest/CUSTOMER/0/">0</\
CUSTOMER>
  <CUSTOMER xlink:href="http://www.thomas-bayer.com/sqlrest/CUSTOMER/1/">1</\
CUSTOMER>
  <CUSTOMER xlink:href="http://www.thomas-bayer.com/sqlrest/CUSTOMER/2/">2</\
CUSTOMER>
</CUSTOMERList>
```

Test script

```
require 'httpclient'
http = HTTPClient.new
resp = http.get("http://www.thomas-bayer.com/sqlrest/CUSTOMER")
puts resp.body
# File.open("C:/temp/rest.xml", "w").puts(resp.body)
xml_doc = REXML::Document.new(resp.body)
expect(xml_doc.root.elements.size).to be > 10
```

The data format returned from this service is XML. In the example, I used REXML, Ruby's built-in XML processor, to analyze the response. The last two statements verify the number of records returned is bigger than 10. For more XML verification, see Chapter 4.

CREATE a record

Create a data record.

Sample Request

URL:	http://www.thomas-bayer.com/sqlrest/CUSTOMER/
HTTP Method:	PUT

Test Script

```
http = HTTPClient.new
create_rest_url = "http://www.thomas-bayer.com/sqlrest/CUSTOMER/"
new_record_xml  = <<END_OF_MESSAGE
<CUSTOMER>
   <ID>66668</ID>
   <FIRSTNAME>Test</FIRSTNAME>
   <LASTNAME>Wise</LASTNAME>
   <STREET>10 Ruby Street</STREET>
   <CITY>Brisbane</CITY>
</CUSTOMER>
END_OF_MESSAGE

resp  = http.put(create_rest_url, new_record_xml)
puts resp.body   # this service: server returns error but actually created OK
```

READ a record

Display a data record.

Sample Request

URL:	http://www.thomas-bayer.com/sqlrest/CUSTOMER/3
HTTP Method:	GET

Sample Response

```
<CUSTOMER xmlns:xlink="http://www.w3.org/1999/xlink">
  <ID>3</ID>
  <FIRSTNAME>Michael</FIRSTNAME>
  <LASTNAME>Clancy</LASTNAME>
  <STREET>542 Upland Pl.</STREET>
  <CITY>San Francisco</CITY>
</CUSTOMER>
```

Test script

```
http = HTTPClient.new
customer_id = 3
get_rest_url = "http://www.thomas-bayer.com/sqlrest/CUSTOMER/#{customer_id}"
resp = http.get(get_rest_url)
puts resp.body
expect(resp.body).to include("<CITY>San Francisco</CITY>")
```

UPDATE a record

Update an existing data record.

Sample Request

URL:	http://www.thomas-bayer.com/sqlrest/CUSTOMER/6666
HTTP Method:	POST

Test script

```
http = HTTPClient.new
cid = 66667
update_rest_url = "http://www.thomas-bayer.com/sqlrest/CUSTOMER/#{cid}/"
update_xml  = <<END_OF_MESSAGE
<CUSTOMER>
   <CITY>Gold Coast</CITY>
</CUSTOMER>
END_OF_MESSAGE
resp  = http.post(update_rest_url, update_xml)
expect(resp.code).to eq(200) # OK
```

DELETE a record

Delete a data record.

Sample Request

URL:	http://www.thomas-bayer.com/sqlrest/CUSTOMER/6666
HTTP Method:	DELETE

Sample Response

```
<resource xmlns:xlink="http://www.w3.org/1999/xlink">
    <deleted>6666</deleted>
</resource>
```

Test script

```
http = HTTPClient.new
cid = 6666 # an existing record
delete_rest_url = "http://www.thomas-bayer.com/sqlrest/CUSTOMER/#{cid}"
resp  = http.delete(delete_rest_url)
# puts resp.body
expect(resp.body).to include("<deleted>6666</deleted>")
```

Using HTTP and REST client: rest-client

REST Client[1] is a HTTP and REST client for Ruby. It is a bit easier to use than Ruby's built-in 'net/http'.

```
gem "rest-client"
require 'rest-client'
response = RestClient.get "http://www.thomas-bayer.com/sqlrest/CUSTOMER"
puts response.code
expect(response.code).to eq(200)
puts response.headers # {:server=>"Apache-Coyote/1.1", :content_type=>"appli\
cation/xml", :date=>"Mon, 28 Dec 2015 01:21:18 GMT", :content_length=>"4574"\
}
puts response.body  # XML
```

 ## Design clean tests

One benefit of automated testing is that the tests can be run very often. The test script below combines "Create" and "Delete" tests into one. If both Create and Delete operations are successful, we can repeatedly run this test.

```
new_record_xml  = <<END_OF_MESSAGE
<CUSTOMER>
        <ID>7777</ID>
        <FIRSTNAME>Clinic</FIRSTNAME>
        <LASTNAME>Wise</LASTNAME>
        <STREET>20 Ruby Street</STREET>
        <CITY>Brisbane</CITY>
</CUSTOMER>
END_OF_MESSAGE

service_url = "http://www.thomas-bayer.com/sqlrest/CUSTOMER"
response = RestClient.put service_url, new_record_xml
puts response.body
```

---

[1]https://github.com/rest-client/rest-client

```
response = RestClient.delete "http://www.thomas-bayer.com/sqlrest/CUSTOMER/7\
777"
expect(response).to include("<deleted>7777</deleted>")
```

CREATE or UPDATE records with dynamic request data

For record-creation automated tests, we usually cannot use the static request data as we might get data already exists error after the first run. The same may apply for record updates. With help of programming, we can use generated dynamic request test data. For example, the test script below updates an existing customer's address.

```
require 'faker' # a library to generate fake data
new_city = Faker::Address.city # randomly generated

response = RestClient.post "http://www.thomas-bayer.com/sqlrest/CUSTOMER/2",\
 "<CUSTOMER><CITY>#{new_city}</CITY></CUSTOMER>"

# verify it is updated
resp_xml = RestClient.get "http://www.thomas-bayer.com/sqlrest/CUSTOMER/2"
expect(resp_xml).to include(new_city)
```

More recipes on request data generation can be found in Chapter 8.

REST web service returns JSON

Unlike SOAP, REST does not have to use XML as the format for the response. Besides XML, REST Web services commonly return messages in JSON (JavaScript Object Notation) format.

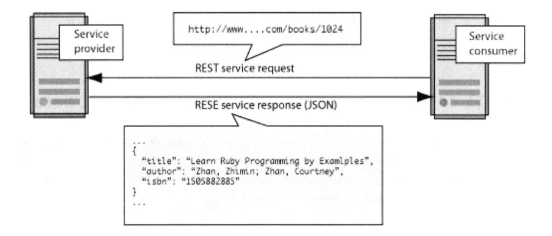

Sample Request

URL: http://api.geonames.org/postalCodeLookupJSON?postalcode=4051&country=AU&username=dem
HTTP Method: GET

Sample Response

```
{
  "postalcodes": [
    {
      "adminCode1": "QLD",
      "adminName2": "NORTHGATE CENT",
      "lng": 153.05817604065,
      "countryCode": "AU",
      "postalcode": "4011",
      "adminName1": "Queensland",
      "placeName": "Clayfield",
      "lat": -27.418938199216
    },
    {
      "adminCode1": "QLD",
      "adminName2": "NORTHGATE CENT",
      "lng": 153.07025481549,
      "countryCode": "AU",
```

```
      "postalcode": "4011",
      "adminName1": "Queensland",
      "placeName": "Hendra",
      "lat": -27.417748174033
    }
  ]
}
```

```
require 'rest-client'
require 'json' # gem install json

# request data
country = "AU"
postcode = "4051"

response = RestClient.get "http://api.geonames.org/postalCodeLookupJSON?post\
alcode=#{postcode}&country=#{country}&username=demo"
json_obj = JSON.parse(response)
expect( json_obj["postalcodes"].collect{|x| x["placeName"]}).to eq(["Alderle\
y", "Enoggera", "Gaythorne", "Grange", "Newmarket", "Wilston"])
```

As you can see, the only difference from testing REST web services return XML is parsing the response in JSON format. I will cover more on data parsing in next chapter.

REST web service sends JSON

Just like REST XML web services, we can use HTTP GET (via a URL) to get a list records or an individual record in JSON, and send JSON messages to create a new record or update an existing one. The scripts below create JSON string in Ruby.

```
new_id = 101
new_title = "Foo"
json_request = <<END_OF_MESSAGE
{
"userId": 1,
"id":  #{new_id},
"title": "#{new_title}",
"body": "some data"
}
END_OF_MESSAGE
```

Here is the output:

```
{
  "userId": 1,
  "id":  101,
  "title": "Foo",
  "body": "some data"
}
```

Using RestClient to invoke HTTP POST method with the above JSON string to create a new record.

```
ws_url = "http://jsonplaceholder.typicode.com/posts"
response = RestClient.post(ws_url, json_request)
expect(response.body).to include("#{new_id}")
```

Or use HTTP PUT or Patch to update an existing resource.

```
json_request.gsub!("101", "10")
response = RestClient.put(ws_url + "/10", json_request)
```

4. Parse Response

Verification in API testing largely is to parse the data returned from API. The common data format used in API response are XML, JSON and CSV. In the chapter, I will show how to parse them in Ruby.

Parse XML with REXML

REXML is a pure XML processor for parsing XML documents. REXML is included in the standard Ruby distribution.

REXML can take a XML string or a XML file as input and parse it into a REXML::Document object.

```ruby
require "rexml/document"

xml_string = <<EOF
<Products>
<Product>TestWise</Product>
<Product>BuildWise</Product>
</Products>
EOF
doc = REXML::Document.new(xml_string)

# from a file
file = File.new(File.join(File.dirname(__FILE__), "../testdata", "books.xml"\
))
doc = REXML::Document.new(file)
```

Here is the sample XML (*books.xml*).

```
<books>
  <category name="Test Automation">
    <book isbn="1505882893">
      <title>Practical Web Test Automation</title>
    </book>
    <book isbn="1505885329">
      <title>Selenium WebDriver Recipes in Ruby</title>
    </book>
  </category>
  <category name="Programming">
    <book isbn="1505882885">
      <title>Learn Ruby Programming by Examples</title>
    </book>
    <book isbn="">
      <title>Learn Swift Programming by Examples</title>
    </book>
  </category>
</books>
```

Parse it with REXML.

```
expect(doc.root.name).to eq("books")
# expect(doc.root.elements["category"].size).to eq(2)

# Creating an array of matching elements
all_book_elems = doc.elements.to_a("//books/category/book/title" )
all_book_titles = all_book_elems.collect{|x| x.text}
expect(all_book_titles).to eq(["Practical Web Test Automation", "Selenium We\
bDriver Recipes in Ruby", "Learn Ruby Programming by Examples", "Learn Swift\
 Programming by Examples"])

# 1-based index
second_book = doc.elements["//book[2]/title"].text
puts second_book   #=> "Selenium WebDriver Recipes in Ruby"

# match first occurrence
first_programming_book = doc.elements["books/category[@name='Programming']/b\
```

```
ook/title"].text
expect(first_programming_book).to eq("Learn Ruby Programming by Examples")
```

XPath, the XML Path Language, is a query language for locating nodes from an XML document. Here is how to use XPath locators in REXML:

```
# Gets an array of all of the "book" elements in the document.
book_elems_array = REXML::XPath.match( doc, "//book" )
expect(book_elems_array.size).to eq(4)

REXML::XPath.each(doc, "//category[@name='Test Automation']/book") { |book_e\
lem|
  puts book_elem.elements["title"].text  # element text
  puts book_elem.attributes["isbn"]      # attribute value
}
```

Parse XML with Nokogiri

Nokogiri[1] is a simple HTML / XML parser in Ruby. Comparing to REXML, Nokogiri has more features and it is fast. I recommend Nokogiri for parsing XML documents.

```
require 'nokogiri' # gem install nokogiri
file = File.new(File.join(File.dirname(__FILE__), "../testdata", "books.xml"\
))
doc = Nokogiri::XML(File.open(file))

expect(doc.xpath("//book").count).to eq(4)
expect(doc.xpath("//book/title")[0].text).to eq("Practical Web Test Automati\
on")
```

Strip out namespaces in XML

Most of the time, there is no need to keep namespaces in XML for verifying XML documents. Nokogiri provides a convenient method to strip the namespaces out.

---

[1]http://www.nokogiri.org/

```ruby
doc = Nokogiri::XML("<a xmlns:x='foo' xmlns:y='bar'><x:b id='1'/><y:b id='2'\
/></a>")
doc.remove_namespaces!
puts doc
```

Output:

```
<a>
  <b id="1"/>
  <b id="2"/>
</a>
```

Please note that Nokogiri also pretty-prints the XML, neat!

Parse XML with Nokogiri in Slop mode

Nokogiri Slop mode offers a more interactive way access nodes and attributes.

```ruby
doc = Nokogiri::Slop(File.read("books.xml"))

expect(doc.books.category[1].book[0].title.content).to eq("Learn Ruby Progra\
mming by Examples")
expect(doc.books.category[0]["name"]).to eq("Test Automation")

# use some xpath
expect(doc.books.category("[@name='Test Automation']").book[1].title.content\
).to eq("Selenium WebDriver Recipes in Ruby")
```

If you like this way and works for you, use it. But be warned, Nokogiri does not recommend using Slop mode[2].

---

[2]http://www.nokogiri.org/tutorials/searching_a_xml_html_document.html#slop_sup_1__sup_

Parse JSON

JSON (JavaScript Object Notation) is a lightweight data-interchange format. JSON gains popularity quickly in recent years as it is concise and easy for human to read (comparing to XML).

The test script below retrieves the live share prices of Yahoo and Apple, and extract "Day Highs/Lows" data.

```ruby
require 'json'
require 'httpclient'
uri = "http://finance.yahoo.com/webservice/v1/symbols/YHOO,AAPL/quote?format\
=json&view=detail"
http = HTTPClient.new
resp = http.get(uri)

json_str = resp.content
```

A sample JSON request.

```json
{
  "list": {
    "meta": {
      "type": "resource-list",
      "start": 0,
      "count": 2
    },
    "resources": [
      {
        "resource": {
          "classname": "Quote",
          "fields": {
            "change": "0.014999",
            "day_high": "33.299999",
            "day_low": "32.689999",
            "name": "Yahoo! Inc.",
            "price": "32.965000",
            "symbol": "YHOO",
```

```
      "utctime": "2015-12-21T21:00:00+0000",
      "volume": "9106706",
    }
  }
},
{
  "resource": {
    "classname": "Quote",
    "fields": {
      "change": "1.300003",
      "day_high": "107.370003",
      "day_low": "105.570000",
      "name": "Apple Inc.",
      "price": "107.330002",
      "symbol": "AAPL",
      "utctime": "2015-12-21T21:00:00+0000",
      "volume": "47590610"
    }
  }
}
]
}
}
```

Parse JSON response

JSON gem, which is often included in a Ruby distribution, provides JSON support in Ruby. If you are familiar with the message structure and accessing elements in Ruby's Hash and Array, parsing JSON is quite easy.

```
require 'json'
json_obj = JSON.parse( json_str )
# puts json_obj.inspect
expect( json_obj["list"]["meta"]["count"] ).to eq(2)
yahoo_share_day_high = json_obj["list"]["resources"][0]["resource"]["fields"\
]["day_low"].to_f
apple_share_day_high = json_obj["list"]["resources"][1]["resource"]["fields"\
]["day_high"].to_f
puts yahoo_share_day_low
puts apple_share_day_high
raise "I wish I bought Apple Share exception" if apple_share_day_high > 150
```

Pretty print JSON

JSON strings returned from API is usually compacted to save communication time. However, this won't be easy for inspecting. (*developing automated test scripts often start with testing it manually*) Pretty-printing JSON can be easily done with JSON gem.

```
json_obj = JSON.parse('{"staff":[ {"firstName":"John", "lastName":"Daw"}, {"\
firstName":"Tom", "lastName":"Jones"}]}')
formatted_json = JSON.pretty_generate(json_obj) # => string
puts formatted_json
File.open("tmp.json", "w").write("formatted_json") # save for inspection
```

Output:

```
{
  "staff": [
    {
      "firstName": "John",
      "lastName": "Daw"
    },
    {
      "firstName": "Tom",
      "lastName": "Jones"
    }
  ]
}
```

Parse CSV

Get the data directly by URL. The example below returns the live currency exchange of Australian Dollar and Japanese Yen.

```
require 'net/http'
yahoo_exchange_rate_live_url = "http://download.finance.yahoo.com/d/quotes.c\
sv?s=AUDJPY=X&f=sl1d1t1ba&e=.csv"
csv_data = Net::HTTP.get(URI.parse(yahoo_exchange_rate_live_url))
```

Sample CSV data returned:

```
"AUDJPY=X",87.2900,"12/22/2015","2:28am",87.2600,87.3200
```

Parse the CSV string using Ruby's built-in CSV library and extract the key data.

```
require 'csv'
csv = CSV.parse(csv_data) # CSV
csv_first_row = csv.shift
exchange_rate = csv_first_row[1].to_f  # => 87.29
puts exchange_rate
```

For more on CSV parsing in Ruby, refer to the Ruby Doc[3].

Parse RSS Feed

RSS (Rich Site Summary) is a XML-based format used for online publishers to deliver regularly changed web content. You may open a RSS URL, such as *http://rss.cnn.com/rss/edition.rss*, in a modern browser. A RSS feed, in essence, is an XML file.

Getting RSS

---

[3]http://ruby-doc.org/stdlib-2.0.0/libdoc/csv/rdoc/CSV.html

```ruby
require 'open-uri'
uri = "http://rss.cnn.com/rss/edition.rss"
rss_xml = Nokogiri.parse(open(uri).read)
```

Here is a sample RSS XML.

```xml
<rss xmlns:dc="http://purl.org/dc/elements/1.1/" xmlns:itunes="http://www.it\
unes.com/dtds/podcast-1.0.dtd" xmlns:media="http://search.yahoo.com/mrss/" x\
mlns:rdf="http://www.w3.org/1999/02/22-rdf-syntax-ns#" xmlns:taxo="http://pu\
rl.org/rss/1.0/modules/taxonomy/" version="2.0">
    <channel>
        <title>CNN.com - Top Stories</title>
        <link>http://edition.cnn.com/index.html?eref=edition</link>
        <!-- ... -->
        <item>
            <title>Human rights lawyer sentence suspended</title>
            <link>http://rss.cnn.com/c/35494/f/676993</link>
            <!-- ... -->
        </item>
        <item>
            <title>Mullah 'killed Afghan-American woman'</title>
            <link>http://rss.cnn.com/c/35494/f/676994</link>
            <!-- ... -->
        </item>
        <!-- ... -->
    </channel>
</rss>
```

Parse RSS

```ruby
require 'nokogiri'
xml_doc = Nokogiri.parse(rss_xml)
xml_doc.remove_namespaces!
# puts xml_doc
top_story_headlines = xml_doc.xpath("//item/title").collect{|x| x.text}
puts top_story_headlines.count # 25
puts top_story_headlines.first # "Donald Trump says ..."
```

 ATOM is another popular web feed format. As far as testing is concerned, it is identical as RSS. An ATOM feed is a XML as well.

Extract pattern text with Regular Expression

Besides parsing data in specific formats, there is a generic and very important skill: **parsing string**. XML, JSON and CSV are all strings. Quite often, we are required to extract a specific piece of data out, like the coupon code in <response>Your coupon code: V7H67U used by 2016-08-18</response>. Regular Expression is an effective and widely used approach for text parsing.

```ruby
coupon_text = "<response>Your coupon code: V7H67U used by 2016-08-18</respon\
se>"
if coupon_text =~ /coupon code:\s+(\w+) used by\s([\d|-]+)/
  coupon_code = $1    # first captures group (\w+)
  expiry_date = $2
  puts "Coupon Code: #{coupon_code}"
  puts "Expire Date: #{expiry_date}"
else
  raise "Error: no valid coupon returned"
end
```

Output:

Regular expression is very powerful and it does take some time to master it. To get it going for simple text matching, however, is not hard. Google 'ruby regular expression' shall return some good tutorials, and Rubular[4] is a helpful tool to let you try out regular expression online.

---

[4]http://rubular.com/

5. Email

Email is an almost certain feature in software applications nowadays. From my observation, email testing often gets neglected in software development for the reasons below:

- Though project managers know emails are important as a main communication channel between the application and end users, during software development, it usually is not considered as the main feature.
- Programmers usually code in testing mode, in which the email delivery is often mocked.
- Testers may find exploratory testing emails is easy: open an email client (such as Outlook), wait and open the email to inspect visually. However, for the same reason, it is easy to miss specific checks. Quite commonly, the emails sent from the application are in one layout, i.e, visually similar.
- Email testing is not performed frequently if done manually. Email checking is often the last step of a sequence of operations on an application. As we know, application changes frequently, therefore email testing shall be performed frequently too.

Testing emails with automated test scripts is the solution.

Send text email - SMTP

Simple Mail Transfer Protocol (SMTP) is a standard for sending emails. Before testing, we need to gather two piece of information:

- SMTP Server name or IP address
- STMP port, default to 25

In the sample script below, it uses Ruby's built-in '**net/smtp**' to send a text email to SMTP server runs on the server **smtp.agileway.net** at port **25**.

```
require 'net/smtp'
raw_message = <<END_OF_MESSAGE
From: AgileWay <mailer@agileway.com.au>
To:  <john@wiseclinic.com>
Subject: Welcome to ClinicWise
Date: Sat, 25 Jul 2015 13:16:42 +1000
Message-Id: <unique.message.id.string@example.com>

Welcome the best online clinic management system.
END_OF_MESSAGE

Net::SMTP.start('smtp.agileway.net', 25) do |smtp|
  smtp.send_message raw_message,
    'mailer@agileway.com.au',     # from
    'john@wiseclinic.com'         # to
end
```

Send HTML email to multiple recipients - SMTP

Sending HTML emails with 'net/smtp' is similar to text emails. For multiple recipients, just put them into an array.

```
html_message = <<MESSAGE_END
From: Agileway Support <support@agileway.com.au>
To: A Test User <test@todomain.com>
MIME-Version: 1.0
Content-type: text/html
Subject: SMTP HTML e-mail test

<h1>This is headline.</h1>
<p>This is <b>HTML</b> message.</p>
MESSAGE_END

Net::SMTP.start('127.0.0.1', 1025) do |smtp|
  smtp.send_message html_message,
    "support@agileway.com.au",
    [ "john@wiseclinic.com", "cc@wiseclinic.com", "bcc@example.org"]
end
```

The email will look like this in email clients:

```
From  <mailer@agileway.com.au>
  To  <john@wiseclinic.com>, <cc@wiseclinic.com>, <bcc@example.org>
Subject  SMTP HTML e-mail test

HTML   Source
```

This is headline.

This is **HTML** message.

Send email with Gmail

Gmail is the most popular email service, it is commonly used for sending test emails. The scripts sends an email with Gmail's SMTP service. To avoid putting plain password in test script, I created an environment variable YOUR_GMAIL_PASSWORD to store the password, then use ENV["YOUR_GMAIL_PASSWORD"] in the script.

```ruby
require 'net/smtp'
message_body = <<END_OF_EMAIL
From: Your Name <agileway@gmail.com>
To: Other Email <other.email@somewhere.com>
Subject: text message

This is a test message.
END_OF_EMAIL

server = 'smtp.gmail.com'
mail_from_domain = 'gmail.com'
port = 587        # or 25 - double check with your provider
username = 'agileway@gmail.com'
password = ENV["YOUR_GMAIL_PASSWORD"]

smtp = Net::SMTP.new(server, port)
smtp.enable_starttls_auto
smtp.start(server, username, password, :plain)
smtp.send_message(message_body, 'support@agileway.com.au')
```

Send email with Mail gem

Sending email using 'Mail' gem is a lot easier, I recommend it.

```ruby
require 'mail'  # gem install mail

Mail.defaults do
  delivery_method :smtp, :address => "127.0.0.1", :port => 1025
end

mail = Mail.new do
  from    'agileway@gmail.com'
  to      'john@wiseclinic.com'
  subject 'Welcome to ClinicWise'
  body    "Wise Choice, ..."
end

mail.deliver
```

Multi-part email with Mail gem

Send Multi-part emails with attachments.

```ruby
mail = Mail.new do
  to      'natalie@wiseclinic.com'
  from    'AgileWay Support <agileway@gmail.com>'
  subject 'First multipart email sent with Mail'

  text_part do
    body 'This is plain text'
  end

  html_part do
    content_type 'text/html; charset=UTF-8'
    body '<h1>This is HTML</h1>'
  end
```

```
end

mail.add_file( File.join(File.dirname(__FILE__), "..", "testdata", "clinicwi\
se_logo.png")  )
mail.add_file( File.join(File.dirname(__FILE__), "..", "testdata", "sample_i\
nvoice.pdf")  )
mail.deliver
```

Check POP3 Email

POP3 (Post Office Protocol 3) is a standard protocol for receiving e-mail. The sample script checks Gmail's POP3 server for new emails.

```
require 'mail'
Mail.defaults do
  retriever_method :pop3,
                   :address    => "pop.gmail.com",
                   :port       => 995,
                   :user_name  => "testwisely01@gmail.com",
                   :password   => ENV["YOUR_GMAIL_PASSWORD"],
                   :enable_ssl => true
end

Mail.first # first unread email
# NOTE: next time you run, it changes as POP3 downloaded will mark as read
debug Mail.first.subject
Mail.last  # last unread email
```

Recently, Gmail added prevention from accessing Gmail using automated scripts like the above one.

```
Sign-in attempt prevented

Someone just tried to sign in to your Google Account testwisely01@gmail.com \
from an app that doesn't meet modern security standards.
```

That is Gmail policy, you might be able to use the script to check emails against your own POP server. But this is not my preferred approach to test incoming emails anyway. During functional (and regression) testing, it is not necessary to send the email out and wait for it to arrive the destination account (this can be in exploratory testing). We just need to make sure the email is sent out conforming the email standard, and then verify the sent email. This will greatly simplify the test setup and time.

Here is how it works: configure the testing SMTP server (can be a fake one) to save incoming emails to files under a specified folder, then perform checks on these files (see the next recipe). An enhanced (and user friendly) approach is that the fake SMTP Server also provides a user interface to see the emails like real email clients, we can write automated test scripts to drive the UI to verify the emails. MailCatcher[1] does just that, I will cover it in Chapter 10.

Verify saved email

EML is a file extension for an e-mail message saved to a file. You can export an email to an EML in your email client, and you also open an EML file in email clients.

Mail[2] gem understands EML format. The samples script below can perform very specific checks against an EML file.

```
require 'mail'  # gem install mail
mail = Mail.read(File.join(File.dirname(__FILE__), "..", "testdata", "messag\
e.eml"))
```

```
puts mail.from              #=> ["agileway@gmail.com"]
puts mail.envelope_from     #=> 'mikel@test.agileway.net'
puts mail.to                #=> ['john@wiseclinic.com']
puts mail.cc                #=>
puts mail.subject           #=> "Welcome to ClinicWise"
puts mail.date.to_s         #=> '2015-08-07T14:16:42+10:00'
puts mail.message_id        #=> '<4D6AA7EB.6490534@xxx.xxx>'
puts mail.body.decoded      #=> 'Wise Choice, ...
```

Verify multi-part email with attachments

---

[1]https://mailcatcher.me/

[2]https://github.com/mikel/mail

```ruby
require 'mail'  # gem install mail
mail = Mail.read(File.join(File.dirname(__FILE__), "..", "testdata", "multip\
art.eml"))

expect(mail.parts.count).to eq(4)
expect(mail.parts[0].body.decoded).to eq("This is plain text")
expect(mail.parts[1].body.decoded).to eq("<h1>This is HTML</h1>")
expect(mail.parts[2].filename).to eq("clinicwise_logo.png")
expect(mail.parts.last.filename).to eq("sample_invoice.pdf")
```

6. Download Binary File

Generally, here are three steps for (binary) file verification.

- Retrieve the file
- Verify a file is downloaded
- Verify the downloaded file is valid for the file type

Download file from static URL

If the binary file URL is static, we jus download it and verify.

```ruby
require 'open-uri'
local_saved_file = File.join(File.dirname(__FILE__), "..", "tmp", "pwta-samp\
le.pdf")
File.open(local_saved_file, "wb") do |saved_file|
  # the following "open" is provided by open-uri
  open("http://samples.leanpub.com/practical-web-test-automation-sample.pdf"\
, "rb") do |read_file|
    saved_file.write(read_file.read)
  end
end
expect(File.exists?(local_saved_file)).to eq(true)
expect(File.size(local_saved_file)).to be > 1400000
```

As automated tests are executed often, we don't want the output of previous test runs to affect the correctness of current test execution. In the context testing file downloading, it is a good practice to make sure the target file is not existing first, like this.

```
local_saved_file = File.join(File.dirname(__FILE__), "..", "tmp", "pwta-samp\
le.pdf")
if File.exists?(local_saved_file)
   require 'fileutils'
   FileUtils.rm(local_saved_file)
end
# then download and verify ....
```

The below is a reusable function to download a file using `httpclient`.

```
def download_file(url, saved_file_path)
  start_time = Time.now

  client = HTTPClient.new
  save_file = File.new(saved_file_path, "wb")
  start_time = Time.now
  save_file.write(client.get_content(url))
  save_file.flush
  save_file.close

  time_to_download = Time.now - start_time
  puts("Time to download => #{time_to_download}")
  return saved_file_path
end
```

The above code above handles redirects.

File download from dynamic URL

To verify a binary file that is a result of a set of operations on application, e.g. checking a receipt PDF of a purchase on an online store, it is more towards functional UI testing than API testing. In this case, we can use Selenium WebDriver to drive the application to complete the payment and download the receipt, then perform PDF checking (see recipes later in the chapter).

Below is a sample Selenium WebDriver script to download a file from Chrome and save it to a specified directory.

```ruby
download_path = RUBY_PLATFORM =~ /mingw/ ? "C:\\TEMP": "/Users/zhimin/tmp"
prefs = {
  :download => {
    :prompt_for_download => false,
    :default_directory => download_path
  }
}
driver = Selenium::WebDriver.for :chrome, :prefs => prefs
driver.navigate.to "http://zhimin.com/books/pwta"
driver.find_element(:link_text, "Download").click
sleep 10 # wait download to complete
expect(File.exists?("#{download_path}/practical-web-test-automation-sample.p\
df")).to be_truthy
driver.quit
```

We will cover the synergy of API and UI testing in Chapter 10.

Verify the file integrity with MD5 or SHA256 Checksum

The standard (and quick) way to verify the integrity of a known file is to compare the checksum, typically with MD5 and SHA256 hash. Ruby has built-in support for both.

```ruby
require 'digest'
file_path = File.join(File.dirname(__FILE__), "../testdata/sample_invoice.p\
df")
md5_hash = Digest::MD5.file(file_path).hexdigest
expect('7eb8022ea779f3288e7cdc0e8aae0745', md5_hash)
sha256_hash = Digest::SHA256.file(file_path).hexdigest
expect("eb90578bfb87698c95165b267f52aaf7ead469e69aa6f23fd92a48fbfe964cbf", s\
ha256_hash)
```

Generate checksum from command line

MD5: `md5 <file_path>`

```
SHA256: shasum -a 256 <file_path>
```

Verify compressed Zip

We can use rubyzip[1] gem to verify a zip file.

```ruby
gem 'rubyzip'
require 'zip'

zip_file_url = "https://testwisely.com/sites/testwisely/books/selenium_recip\
es/selenium-recipes-sample-source.zip"
saved_file_path = download_file(zip_file_url, "selenium-recipes-sample-sourc\
e.zip")
zip_file_io = Zip::File.open(saved_file_path)
all_file_list = []
zip_file_io.each do |entry|
  all_file_list << entry.name
end
expect(all_file_list).to include("selenium-recipes-sample-source/ch01_open_c\
hrome.rb")
```

Invalid zip file

```ruby
begin
  bad_zip_path = File.join(File.dirname(__FILE__), "../testdata/bad.zip")
  Zip::File.open(bad_zip_path)
rescue => e
  puts e.message
  expect(e.message).to include("can't dup NilClass")
end
```

---

[1]https://github.com/rubyzip/rubyzip

Verify PDF

PDF (Portable Document Format) probably is the most common binary file type that requires verification during testing. By using pdf-reader[2] gem, we could check whether the downloaded file is a valid PDF or not. PDF may contain metadata. If the document generator utilizes the metadata, this makes the verification in testing much easier and more specific.

```ruby
pdf_url = "http://samples.leanpub.com/practical-web-test-automation-sample.p\
df"
saved_file_path = download_file(pdf_url, "pwta.pdf")

require 'pdf-reader' # gem install pdf-reader
fio = File.open(saved_file_path, "rb")
reader = PDF::Reader.new(fio)
pdf_metadata = reader.info
puts pdf_metadata
expect(pdf_metadata[:Author]).to eq("Zhimin Zhan")
expect(pdf_metadata[:Title]).to eq("Practical Web Test Automation")
```

Invalid PDF file

```ruby
begin
  bad_pdf_path = File.join(File.dirname(__FILE__), "../testdata/bad.pdf")
  reader = PDF::Reader.new(File.open(bad_pdf_path, "rb"))
rescue => e
  puts e.message
  # depends on data, the error might be different
  expect(e.message).to include("xref table not found")
end
```

Verify downloaded Excel file

To read and write Microsoft Excel compatible spreadsheets, we can use spreadsheet[3] gem.

---

[2]https://github.com/yob/pdf-reader
[3]https://github.com/zdavatz/spreadsheet

```
require 'spreadsheet' # gem install spreadsheet
# more info, https://github.com/zdavatz/spreadsheet/blob/master/GUIDE.md

pdf_path = File.join(File.dirname(__FILE__), "../testdata/users.xls")
book = Spreadsheet.open(pdf_path)
expect(book.worksheets.size).to eq(1)
expect(book.worksheets.first.name).to eq("users")

puts book.worksheets[0].rows.count  # => 5
expect(book.worksheets[0].rows[1][2]).to eq("testwise")
```

Bad Excel File

```
begin
  bad_xls_path = File.join(File.dirname(__FILE__), "../testdata/bad.xls")
  book = Spreadsheet.open(bad_xls_path)
rescue => e
  puts e.message
  # depends on data, the error might be different
  expect(e.message).to include("broken allocationtable chain")
end
```

Verify PNG

Like PDF, a PNG file can contain metadata, which can be used for assertion. ChunkyPNG[4] is a
library that can read and write PNG files.

---

[4]https://github.com/wvanbergen/chunky_png

```
require 'chunky_png'
png_image_url = "https://s3.amazonaws.com/titlepages.leanpub.com/selenium-re\
cipes-in-ruby/hero?1427192483"
saved_file_path = download_file(png_image_url, "selenium_recipes.png")

image = ChunkyPNG::Image.from_file(saved_file_path)
# puts image.metadata.inspect
puts image.metadata["date:create"] # eg. 2015-07-05T10:40:28+00:00
```

You may use freeware TweakPNG[5] to verify the PNG image's metadata in visual manner.

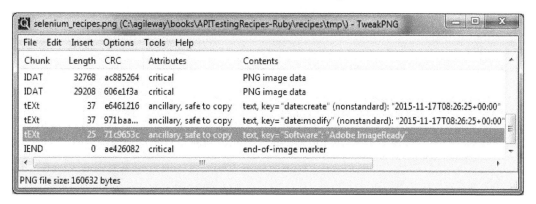

Bad PNG file

```
begin
  bad_png_path = File.join(File.dirname(__FILE__), "../testdata/bad.png")
  image = ChunkyPNG::Image.from_file(bad_png_path)
rescue => e
  puts e.message
  expect(e.message).to include("Chuck CRC mismatch!")
end
```

---

[5]http://entropymine.com/jason/tweakpng/

7. Database

For database-backed applications, the ultimate way to obtain accurate test data and perform verification is to interact with the database directly. For many projects, this might not be possible. For ones do, this provides the ultimate flexibility. Obviously, SQL (Structured Query Language) knowledge is required.

SQLite

Sqlite[1] is often embedded with application due to its simplicity: single-file cross-platform Database. According to its homepage, Sqlite is the "most widely deployed"[2] database engine in the world.

The official gem to interact with a Sqlite database is **Sqlite3**[3]. The sample test script below opens a SQLite database (a file) to get the oldest user in users table.

```ruby
require 'sqlite3' # gem install sqlite3
db = SQLite3::Database.new File.join(File.dirname(__FILE__), "..", "testdata\
", "sample.db")

# Users table: with login, name, age
oldest_user_login = nil
db.execute( "select * from users order by age desc" ) do |row|
  oldest_user_login = row[0]
  break
end

expect(oldest_user_login).to eq("mark")
```

---

[1]https://www.sqlite.org/
[2]https://www.sqlite.org/mostdeployed.html
[3]https://github.com/sparklemotion/sqlite3-ruby

MySQL

MySQL is the most widely used open-source client–server model relational databases[4]. The gem for accessing MySQL is Mysql2[5] (mysql is the old one, which has been deprecated).

The test script below queries the database for the longest build time in builds table.

```
require 'mysql2'  # gem install mysql2
client = Mysql2::Client.new(:host => "10.0.0.1",
                            :username => "tester",
                            :password => "wise",
                            :database => "buildwise_production")
results = client.query("SELECT duration FROM builds WHERE project_id=3 ORDER\
 BY duration DESC")
headers = results.fields # <= that's an array of field names, in order
puts headers # => ["duration"]
longest_build_time = nil
results.each do |row|
  longest_build_time = row["duration"]
  break
end
puts longest_build_time
```

Please note that row[:duration] won't work unless you add :symbolize_keys => true into the query()'s parameters.

Don't save credentials in test scripts

It is OK to use a test user's password (for login) plainly in test scripts, but not for sensitive data such as database credentials. A good approach is to define sensitive data in environment variables, and use them in the test scripts.

```
client = Mysql2::Client.new(:host => "10.0.0.1",
                            :username => ENV["DB_USER"],
                            :password => ENV["DB_PASS"],
                            :database => "buildwise_production")
```

---

[4]http://www.oracle.com/us/products/mysql/overview/index.html
[5]https://github.com/brianmario/mysql2

PostgreSQL

PostgreSQL[6], often called Postgres, is another popular open-source database. The gem for interactive with Postgres is pg[7].

```ruby
gem "pg"  # gem install pg
require 'pg'

conn = PG.connect( :host  => "127.0.0.1",
                   :port     => 5432,
                   :user     => "postgres",
                   :password => "test",
                   :dbname => 'buildwise_production' )
conn.exec( "SELECT * FROM pg_stat_activity" ) do |result|
  puts "      PID | User             | Query"
  result.each do |row|
    puts " %7d | %-16s | %s " %
      row.values_at('procpid', 'usename', 'current_query')
  end
end
```

MS SQL server

Microsoft SQL Server[8] is the default database for .NET platform, it is probably the most widely used commercial database. The gem for interacting with SQL Server is TinyTDS[9].

---

[6]http://www.postgresql.org/
[7]https://bitbucket.org/ged/ruby-pg/wiki/Home
[8]https://www.microsoft.com/en-us/server-cloud/products/sql-server/
[9]https://github.com/rails-sqlserver/tiny_tds

```
require 'tiny_tds' # gem install tiny_tds
client = TinyTds::Client.new(:username => 'sa',
                             :password => ENV["DB_PASS"], # set it in enviro\
nment variables,
                             :host => 'myhost.com',
                             :database => "mydb")
result = client.execute("SELECT * FROM USERS where clinic_id = 9")
result.each do |row|
    # row.inspect  =>  e.g {"Id" => 1, "Name" => "James"}
    # By default each row is a hash.
    # The keys are the fields, as you'd expect.
    # The values are pre-built Ruby primitives mapped from their correspondi\
ng types.
end

client.close
```

Easier Database Interaction with ActiveRecord

Writing SQLs can be a headache for some testers, or even developers. ActiveRecord[10] can dramatically simplify this task. ActiveRecord is one of widely used gem for database access, as it is released as a part of the popular Ruby on Rails framework. Here are the steps to use it in your test scripts:

1. Define model class extends form ActiveRecord

   ```
   class YourModel < ActiveRecord::Base
   end
   ```

   By default, the model is mapped the table names as illustrated below:

Model / Class	Table / Schema
Article	articles
LineItem	line_items
Person	people

---

[10]https://github.com/rails/rails/tree/master/activerecord

However, you can customize the table name for your model.

```
class User < ActiveRecord::Base
  self.table_name = "customer"
end
```

2. Set up database connection

```
ActiveRecord::Base.establish_connection( ... )
```

3. Use Active Record Query Interface[11] in test scripts to interact with the database

```
Model.count # return total rows of this database
Model.find(10).name # the name column of the record with ID equal to 10
Model.last  # the last record
Model.where(:author => "Zhimin Zhan").order("publish_date DESC") # query
Model.where("orders_count = ? AND locked = ?", 2, false) # query
```

There is a lot more you can do, such as execute raw SQLs:

```
ActiveRecord::Base.connection.execute("SELECT * FROM users")
ActiveRecord::Base.connection.execute("INSERT INTO ...")
```

4. Close database connection

```
ActiveRecord::Base.connection.close
```

Here is a complete test script that use ActiveRecord to perform database verification.

```
require 'active_record' # gem install activerecord

class Build < ActiveRecord::Base
end

describe "Database with ActiveRecord" do

  before(:all) do
    require 'mysql2'        # gem install mysql2
```

---

[11]http://guides.rubyonrails.org/active_record_querying.html

```
  ActiveRecord::Base.establish_connection(
    :adapter  => 'mysql2', # or 'postgresql' or 'sqlite3'
    :database => 'buildwise_production',
    :username => 'root',
    :password => ENV["MYSQL_PASSWORD"] || "",
    :host =>      'localhost'
  )
end


after(:all) do
  ActiveRecord::Base.connection.close
end



it "ActiveRecord to check database" do
  puts Build.count
  longest_build = Build.order("duration desc").first
  puts longest_build.inspect # find out data
  puts longest_build.duration
end


end
```

Thanks to ActiveRecord and the beautiful ruby language, the test script syntax is a lot simpler, no SQL and the scripts to iterates result sets.

before(:all) and after(:all are two blocks of scripts that run before and after all test cases in RSpec. We open a database connection in before(:all) and close it in after(:all), a common programming idiom for dealing with database connections.

Query With Association

To query database tables with association, we use JOINs in SQL. However, this can get quite complex. Frankly speaking, I don't have some confidence on myself. ActiveRecord can help on that.

Following the example above, we want to get the name of project that has longest build time, here is the test scrip using ActiveRecord, without SQL joins.

```ruby
class Project < ActiveRecord::Base
end

class Build < ActiveRecord::Base
  belong_to :project
end

# ...

  it "ActiveRecord Association" do
    the_project = Build.order("duration desc").first.project
    expect(the_project.name).to eq("ClinicWise")
  end
```

In ActiveRecord, `belongs_to` sets up the association between `Build` and `Project`, it is just that simple. We then can use `a_build.project` to get a build's associated project.

8. Generate Request Data

We have seen using data templates to generate data, such as SOAP requests. Within the template, we often need to generate specific data items such as today's date, unique email, person name, ..., etc.

Generate dynamic dates

```ruby
require 'date' # only need to require once

# assume today is 2016-05-25
Date.today.strftime("%m/%d/%Y") # => 05/25/2016
(Time.now + 1 * 24 * 3600).strftime("%Y-%m-%d %H:%M") # => 2016-05-27 19:57
```

By using ActiveSupport[1] extension, we can generate more flexible dates in a very readable form.

```ruby
# gem install activesupport
require 'active_support/all'

Date.today                    # 2016-07-25
Date.today.tomorrow()         # 2016-07-26
Date.today.next_week()        # 2016-08-01
Date.today.month()            # 2016-08-25
Date.today.end_of_week        # 2016-07-31
2.days.ago(Date.today)        # 2016-07-23
3.days.since(Date.today)      # 2016-07-28
```

Visit the doc[2] for more usage.

---

[1]https://github.com/rails/rails/tree/master/activesupport
[2]http://api.rubyonrails.org/v2.3/classes/ActiveSupport/CoreExtensions/Date/Calculations.html#M001085

Generate random boolean value

Boolean has two values: true and false. Despite of its simplicity, flexible use of random boolean value can empower your test script greatly. For example, for testing a user registration feature, I could write two test cases for genders: "Male" and "Female". If verifying the gender is not the key part of the requirement, I could just write one test cases that fills the gender randomly.

```ruby
rand(2) == 1  # => true or false
random_gender = (rand(2) == 1 ? "male" : "female")
puts random_gender # male or female
```

Generate random number

```ruby
rand()          # a real time between 0 and 1, eg 0.05619897760265391
(rand(90) + 10) # a number between 10 and 99
```

The use of this technique can be extended to generate random character, strings and others.

Generate name and address

Faker[3] is a library generates random test data.

```ruby
require 'faker'
Faker::Name.name # => "Jeromy Erdman"
Faker::Name.first_name # => "Maverick"
Faker::Internet.email # => "jamarcus@kertzmann.com"
Faker::Address.street_address # => "290 Nienow Flats"
Faker::PhoneNumber.phone_number # => "621 Wuckert Plaza"
```

We can further customize by using Ruby's string methods. The scripts below will return a name up to 10 characters, all in lower case.

---

[3]https://github.com/stympy/faker

```ruby
new_name = Faker::Name.name
puts new_name                   # Vernie Dare
puts new_name.downcase[0..9]    # vernie dar
new_name.downcase[0..9].gsub(" ", "-")   # => vernie-dar
```

General unique IDs

One automated test will be run against the same server many times. This is the nature of test automation. If there is ID involved, most of the time, we want them to be unique. Otherwise, we will get unexpected side effects.

```ruby
# A random number at fixed length
# not guarantee unique but unlikely to have duplicate
rand(899999999) + 100000000  # 9 digits


# UUID (Universally Unique Identifier)
require 'securerandom' # included in Ruby
SecureRandom.uuid #=> a77e84e6-f9b3-42cb-bf17-4369c872986b
SecureRandom.uuid #=> f45fc2a8-e272-4bb4-b36e-39d4fe410e3a


require 'faker'  # gem install faker
# a uniq ID
Faker::Bitcoin.address # => 1MoE1F5X5aP4yxWYnYJZfw2JXHruuSUTSh
Faker::Bitcoin.address # => 13NRmmntobsrKhzXrC5YEJauoYyvwefNp8
```

Generate test files at specific size

```ruby
require 'fileutils'
tmp_dir = File.join(File.dirname(__FILE__), "tmp")
FileUtils.mkdir(tmp_dir) unless File.exists?(tmp_dir)
File.open(File.join(tmp_dir, "2MB.txt"), "w") {|f|
  f.write( '0' * 1024 * 1024 * 2 )
}
```

Generate various text files from templates

In Chapter 2, I showed one recipe to generate SOAP request XML from a template. This approach can be applied to any text messages, and I use it often. As it is important, here I will show another example: generate a JSON request for testing REST web services using a template.

Here is a sample XML, which I get from calling a REST GET web service.

```
{
  "userId": 1,
  "id":   101,
  "title": "Foo",
  "body": "some data"
}
```

Then I create an ERB template based on it, and save it in the file: *sample_json.erb*.

```
{
  "userId": <%= @user_id || 1 %>,
  "id": <%= @id %>,
  "title": "<%= @title %>",
  "body": "<%= @body %>"
}
```

 ### Default value in one statement

In Ruby, we can supply the default value in one statement, like `@user_id || 1`. This will avoid unexpected errors if a value is not set.

```
@user_id = nil
@user_id || 1   # => 1
@user_id = 23
@user_id || 1   # => 23
```

The test scripts below use the template to generate three JSON messages and verify the Create operation of a Restful web service.

```
ws_url = "http://jsonplaceholder.typicode.com/posts"
template_file = File.join(File.dirname(__FILE__), "../data/sample_json.erb")
json_erb = ERB.new(File.read(template_file))

(101..103).each do |id|
  @id = id
  @title = "Foo#{id}"
  @body = "Bar#{id}"
  json_request = json_erb.result(binding)
  # puts json_request
  response = RestClient.post(ws_url, json_request)
  expect(response.body).to include("#{@id}")
end
```

Error handling in ERB templates

The use of templates such as ERB can be applied generally to generate text data such as JSON, HTML or XML. The text in <% %> is considered as ruby code. If it is code, it may have error scenarios. For example, the below in a ERB template is trying to generate a name from two instance variables @first_name and @last_name.

```
Name: <%= @first_name + " " + @last_name %>
```

However, if @first_name is not set, the template will throw error: *"NoMethodError: undefined method '+' for nil:NilClass"*. A concise way to catch the error is to add rescue with default value.

```
Name: <%= (@first_name + " " + @last_name) rescue "Not supplied" %>
```

Generate XML

We can use generic ERB template approach to generate XMLs. For simple XML, I found builder[4] is simpler.

---

[4]https://github.com/jimweirich/builder

```ruby
gem "builder"      # gem install builder
require 'builder'
builder = Builder::XmlMarkup.new
xml = builder.person { |b|
    b.name("James Bond", :age => 40)
    b.phone("789-1234")
}
puts xml
```

Output:

```
<person><name age="40">James Bond</name><phone>789-1234</phone></person>
```

Modify existing XML

```ruby
require 'nokogiri'
xml_string = <<EOF
<Products>
<Product version="1.5.5">BuildWise</Product>
<Product version="4">TestWise</Product>
</Products>
EOF
doc = Nokogiri::XML(xml_string)
elem = doc.xpath("//Product[text()='TestWise']")[0]
elem.content = "TestWise IDE"
elem["version"] = "1.6"
expect(doc.to_xml).to include('<Product version="1.6">TestWise IDE</Product>\
')
```

We can also add or remove nodes.

```
buildwise_elem = doc.xpath("//Product[text()='BuildWise']")
buildwise_elem.remove
expect(doc.to_xml).not_to include('<Product>BuildWise</Product>')

products_node =  doc.xpath("//Products")[0]
new_note = Nokogiri::XML::Node.new "Product", products_node
new_note.content = "ClinicWise"
products_node.children.last.add_next_sibling(new_note)
puts doc.to_s
```

Final XML:

```
<?xml version="1.0"?>
<Products>
  <Product version="1.6">TestWise IDE</Product>
  <Product>ClinicWise</Product>
</Products>
```

Generate JSON

```
require 'json'
results = {}
results["count"] = 2
months = { "English" => ["January", "February"], "Chinese" => ["1yue", "2yue\
"] }
results["locale"] = months
puts results.to_json
```

```
{"count":2,"locale":{"English":["January","February"],"Chinese":["1yue","2yu\
e"]}}
```

Modify existing JSON

```ruby
require 'json'
json_obj = JSON.parse('{"staff":[ {"firstName":"John", "lastName":"Daw"}, {"\
firstName":"Tom", "lastName":"Jones"}]}')
json_obj["staff"][0]["lastName"] = "Foo"
json_obj["staff"].delete_at(1) # remove the second one
expect(json_obj.to_json).not_to include('Jones')

json_obj["staff"] << {"firstName" => "New", "lastName" => "One"}
puts json_obj.to_json
```

Output:

```
{
  "staff": [
    {
      "firstName": "John",
      "lastName": "Foo"
    },
    {
      "firstName": "New",
      "lastName": "One"
    }
  ]
}
```

Generate JSON with model

Sometimes, the request data we need to generate is complex, a flat name-value pair is hard to manage. In this case, I would create models for the data. This is a powerful concept and quite practical too. For example, our App A is integrating an third party app B. To effectively test our app to respond the requests from B, we need a certain level of ability to simulate B. In my opinion, the best approach is to create our own models for B. This might sound complex and scary. Fortunately, with Ruby it is not that hard, and I have used this approach regularly. Here is an example.

The model classes:

```ruby
require 'active_support/all'

class Book
  attr_accessor :title
  attr_accessor :isbn
  attr_accessor :isbn_13
  attr_accessor :authors

  def initialize
    @authors = []
  end

  def to_json(opts = {})
    hash = {
      "title" => @title,
      "isbn" =>  @isbn,
      "authors" => @authors.as_json()
    }
    return hash.to_json
  end

end

class Author
  attr_accessor :first_name
  attr_accessor :last_name
  attr_accessor :gender

  def as_json(opts = {})
    hash = {
      "first_name" =>  @first_name,
      "last_name" =>  @last_name
    }
    return hash
  end

end
```

Construct the object and export it to JSON.

```
a_book = Book.new
a_book.title = "Practical Web Test Automation"
a_book.isbn = "1505882893"

author = Author.new
author.first_name = "Zhimin"
author.last_name = "Zhan"
a_book.authors << author

another_author = Author.new
another_author.first_name = "Steve"
another_author.last_name = "Apple"
a_book.authors << another_author

puts a_book.to_json
```

Output:

```
{
  "title": "Practical Web Test Automation",
  "isbn": "1505882893",
  "authors": [
    {
      "first_name": "Zhimin",
      "last_name": "Zhan"
    },
    {
      "first_name": "Steve",
      "last_name": "Apple"
    }
  ]
}
```

Generate Zip file

In Chapter 6, I use `rubyzip` gem to verify a downloaded zip file. We can also use `rubyzip` to generate a compressed zip file for a folder or a set of files. For zip file generation, I prefer `archive/zip` for its simple syntax. Here is an example.

```ruby
require 'archive/zip' # gem install archive-zip
# Add a_directory and its contents to testdata.zip.
data_dir = File.join(File.dirname(__FILE__), "../testdata")
ouptut_zip_file = File.join(File.dirname(__FILE__), "../tmp", "testdata.zip")
Archive::Zip.archive(ouptut_zip_file, data_dir)
expect(File.exists?(ouptut_zip_file)).to be_truthy
```

Generate CSV file

Ruby has a built-in CSV library for parsing and generating CSV files.

```ruby
require "CSV"
tmp_dir = File.join(File.dirname(__FILE__), "tmp")
FileUtils.mkdir(tmp_dir) unless File.exists?(tmp_dir)
CSV.open(File.join(tmp_dir, "clinicwise_pricing.csv"), "wb") do |csv|
  csv << ["Plan", "Practitioner Count", "Price per month"]
  csv << ["Solo", "1", "$35.00"]
  csv << ["Team", "5", "$65.00"]
end
```

Generate Excel file with spreadsheet

We can spreadsheet[5] to create and modify Excel files.

---

[5]https://github.com/zdavatz/spreadsheet

```ruby
require 'spreadsheet'  # gem install spreadsheet
book = Spreadsheet::Workbook.new
sheet_1 = book.create_worksheet(:name => "ClinicWise")
sheet_1.row(0).push "Practitioner Count", "Monthly Price"
sheet_1.row(1).push 1, 35
sheet_1.row(2).push 5, 65
sheet_2 = book.create_worksheet(:name => "SiteWise CMS")
sheet_2.row(0).push "Service", "Price"
sheet_2.row(1).push "Set up", 499
sheet_2.row(2).push "Monthly on-going", 35
tmp_dir = File.join(File.dirname(__FILE__), "tmp")
FileUtils.mkdir(tmp_dir) unless File.exists?(tmp_dir)
book.write File.join(tmp_dir, "products.xls")
```

Generate Excel file with spreadsheet

We can use spreadsheet[6] gem to create and modify Excel files.

```ruby
require 'spreadsheet'  # gem install spreadsheet
book = Spreadsheet::Workbook.new
sheet_1 = book.create_worksheet(:name => "ClinicWise")
sheet_1.row(0).push "Practitioner Count", "Monthly Price"
sheet_1.row(1).push 1, 35
sheet_1.row(2).push 5, 65
sheet_2 = book.create_worksheet(:name => "SiteWise CMS")
sheet_2.row(0).push "Service", "Price"
sheet_2.row(1).push "Set up", 499
sheet_2.row(2).push "Monthly on-going", 35
tmp_dir = File.join(File.dirname(__FILE__), "tmp")
FileUtils.mkdir(tmp_dir) unless File.exists?(tmp_dir)
book.write File.join(tmp_dir, "products.xls")
```

Generate open XML spreadsheet with templates

Open XML spreadsheet is a file format used by Microsoft Excel with extension .xlsx. XLSX file, in essence, is a XML file. Here I introduce an alternative way: using ERB template to

---

[6]https://github.com/zdavatz/spreadsheet

generate spreadsheet document that can be opened in Excel.

Open XML Spreadsheet Template

Mainly three sections:

- <Styles> : The definitions of styles than can by applied to cells.
- <Column>: define columns including widths
- <Row>: Row data

```xml
<?xml version="1.0"?>
<Workbook xmlns="urn:schemas-microsoft-com:office:spreadsheet"
  xmlns:o="urn:schemas-microsoft-com:office:office"
  xmlns:x="urn:schemas-microsoft-com:office:excel"
  xmlns:ss="urn:schemas-microsoft-com:office:spreadsheet"
  xmlns:html="http://www.w3.org/TR/REC-html40">
  <ss:Styles>
    <Style ss:ID="s22">
      <Font ss:Size="13" />
      <NumberFormat ss:Format="yyyy\-mm\-dd"/>
    </Style>
    <Style ss:ID="s1"><Font ss:Bold="1"/></Style>
    <Style ss:ID="s2"><Font ss:Size="13" /></Style>
    <Style ss:ID="s4">
     <Borders>
      <Border ss:Position="Bottom" ss:LineStyle="Continuous" ss:Weight="1"/>
      <Border ss:Position="Left" ss:LineStyle="Continuous" ss:Weight="1"/>
      <Border ss:Position="Right" ss:LineStyle="Continuous" ss:Weight="1"/>
      <Border ss:Position="Top" ss:LineStyle="Continuous" ss:Weight="1"/>
     </Borders>
     <Font x:Family="Swiss" ss:Size="14"  ss:Bold="1"/>
     <Interior ss:Color="#CCFFFF" ss:Pattern="Solid"/>
    </Style>
    <Style ss:ID="s8">
     <Alignment ss:Horizontal="Center" ss:Vertical="Bottom"/>
     <Font x:Family="Swiss" ss:Size="24" ss:Bold="1"/>
    </Style>
    <Style ss:ID="s23" ss:Name="Currency">
```

```
    <Font ss:Size="13" />
    <NumberFormat ss:Format="Currency"/>
  </Style>
</ss:Styles>
<Worksheet ss:Name="Sheet1">
  <Table >
    <Column ss:AutoFitWidth="0" ss:Width="82"/>
    <Column ss:AutoFitWidth="0" ss:Width="90"/>
    <Column ss:AutoFitWidth="0" ss:Width="148"/>
    <Column ss:AutoFitWidth="0" ss:Width="90"/>
    <Column ss:AutoFitWidth="0" ss:Width="90"/>
    <Row ss:Height="30">
      <Cell ss:MergeAcross="5" ss:StyleID="s8"><Data ss:Type="String">Invo\
ices Report</Data></Cell>
    </Row>


    <Row ss:Height="24"  ss:StyleID="s1">
      <Cell ss:MergeAcross="2" ss:StyleID="s2" ><Data ss:Type="String"><%=\
@starts_at.strftime('%Y-%m-%d') %> to <%= @ends_at.strftime('%Y-%m-%d') %><\
/Data></Cell>
        <Cell ss:StyleID="s2" ><Data ss:Type="String"><%= @invoices.count %>\
 Invoices</Data></Cell>
        <Cell ss:MergeAcross="2" ss:StyleID="s2"><Data ss:Type="String">Tota\
l Amount: $<%= @total_invoice_amount %></Data></Cell>
    </Row>


    <Row ss:Height="20">
      <Cell ss:StyleID="s4"><Data ss:Type="String">Invoice Ref</Data></Cel\
l>
        <Cell ss:StyleID="s4"><Data ss:Type="String">Invoice Date</Data></Ce\
ll>
        <Cell ss:StyleID="s4"><Data ss:Type="String">Client</Data></Cell>
        <Cell ss:StyleID="s4"><Data ss:Type="String">Amount</Data></Cell>
        <Cell ss:StyleID="s4"><Data ss:Type="String">Comments</Data></Cell>
    </Row>
    <% @invoices.each do |inv| %>
    <Row   ss:StyleID="s2" ss:Height="18"  >
      <Cell><Data ss:Type="Number"><%= inv.reference_number %></Data></Cel\
```

```
l>
        <Cell ss:StyleID="s22"><Data ss:Type="DateTime"><%= inv.invoice_date\
.strftime("%Y-%m-%d") rescue nil %></Data></Cell>
        <Cell><Data ss:Type="String"><%= inv.client %></Data></Cell>
        <Cell ss:StyleID="s23"><Data ss:Type="Number"><%= inv.total_price  %\
></Data></Cell>
        <Cell><Data ss:Type="String"><%= inv.comments %></Data></Cell>
      </Row>
    <% end %>


    </Table>
  </Worksheet>
</Workbook>
```

Test Script

I put the below techniques into this single test:

- Generate dynamic dates
- Formatting dates
- Random numbers
- Random names
- Use of ERB templates
- Use of Models to prepare test data

```ruby
# The model class
class Invoice
  attr_accessor :reference_number, :invoice_date, :client, :total_price
  attr_accessor :comments
end

# ...

it "Generate Open XML Spreadsheet with templates " do
  require 'erb'
  require 'active_support/all'
  require 'faker'
```

```ruby
  # create template
  template = File.join(File.dirname(__FILE__), "../testdata", "template.xlsx\
.erb")
  erb = ERB.new(File.read(template))

  # set / generate test data
  @starts_at = 7.days.ago(Date.today).beginning_of_week
  @ends_at =  @starts_at.end_of_week
  @invoices = []

  @total_invoice_amount = 0
  10.times do |id|
    an_invoice = Invoice.new
    an_invoice.reference_number = (1000 + id).to_s.rjust(4, "0")
    an_invoice.client = Faker::Name.name
    an_invoice.invoice_date = rand(7).to_i.days.since(@starts_at)
    an_invoice.total_price = rand(3000)  + 10
    @total_invoice_amount +=  an_invoice.total_price
    an_invoice.comments = ""
    @invoices << an_invoice
  end

  # apply template generation and save to file
  dest_file = File.join(File.dirname(__FILE__), "../tmp", "invoices.xls")
  the_output = erb.result(binding)
  debug "=> " + the_output
  File.open(dest_file, "w").write(the_output)
end
```

Generated excel document opened in Excel:

	G1		⊗ ⊘	fx		
	A	B	C	D	E	F

Invoices Report

2016-07-18 to 2016-07-24			10 Invoices	Total Amount: $13626	
Invoice Ref	**Invoice Date**	**Client**	**Amount**	**Comments**	
1000	2016-07-20	Sallie Marquardt	$1,228.00		
1001	2016-07-18	Jaida Friesen	$612.00		
1002	2016-07-18	Burdette Greenfelder	$186.00		
1003	2016-07-24	Hailee Deckow	$1,554.00		
1004	2016-07-24	Rafaela Treutel	$2,547.00		
1005	2016-07-23	Mr. Earnestine Reilly	$2,616.00		
1006	2016-07-23	Marilyne Jacobson MD	$2,058.00		
1007	2016-07-23	Crawford Langosh PhD	$1,513.00		
1008	2016-07-19	Mohammed Renner	$701.00		
1009	2016-07-18	Rudy Fay	$611.00		

9. Headless HTML

HTML is what behind web pages, which we can use Selenium WebDriver to drive in browser to perform testing. Under certain circumstances, for example, the machine is running headless mode, we want to get some data from a web site but performing UI testing is not possible.

Parse HTML with Nokogiri

We could retrieve the HTML and parse them like XML using Nokogiri.

```
html_str = <<EOF
<html><head><title>Hello World</title></head>
<body>
    <h1>This is an awesome document</h1><input type="hidden" name="locale" v\
alue="en-AU">
<p>
  This is a <b>bold</b> paragraph. <br>
    <a id="a-link" href="http://google.ca">I am a link</a>
</p>
</body></html>
EOF

doc = Nokogiri::HTML(html_str)
puts doc.to_xhtml
expect(doc.css("#a-link").text).to eq("I am a link")
expect(doc.css("b").text).to eq("bold")
expect(doc.css("input[name='locale']")[0]["value"]).to eq("en-AU")
```

The below is an example to get the page source (HTML) from a web page and parse it.

```ruby
require 'open-uri'
page = Nokogiri::HTML(open("http://travel.agileway.net"))
links = page.css("a")
expect(links.size)
expect(links[1].text).to eq("Login")
```

Headless web browsing with Mechanize and parse HTML

```ruby
require 'mechanize'  # gem install mechanize
agent = Mechanize.new
home_page = agent.get 'http://travel.agileway.net'

flight_page = home_page.form_with(:action => '/sessions') do |f|
  f.username = "agileway"  # set form name
  f.password = "testwise"
end.submit

passenger_page = flight_page.form_with(:action => "/flights/select_date") do\
 |f|
  f.fromPort = "Sydney"  # dropdown
  f.toPort = "New York"
end.submit

payment_page = passenger_page.form_with(:action => "/flights/passenger") do \
 |f|
  f.passengerFirstName = "Bob"
  f.passengerLastName  = "Tester"
end.submit

expect(payment_page.form_with(:action => "/payment/confirm").holder_name).to\
 eq("Bob Tester")
```

Manage Cookies

```ruby
http = Net::HTTP.new('testwisely.com', 443)
http.use_ssl = true
http.verify_mode = OpenSSL::SSL::VERIFY_NONE # Ignore SSL error
buy_buildwise_agent_path = "/carts/add_product?code=BWAS20"
buy_testwise_path = "/carts/add_product?code=TWNA01"
cart_path = "/shopping/cart"

# make a request to get the server's cookies
response = http.get(buy_buildwise_agent_path)
if response.code == "301" || response.code == "302" # redirect
  all_cookies = response.get_fields('set-cookie')
  # debug all_cookies
  cookies_array = Array.new    # compose a cookie object
  all_cookies.each { | cookie |
    cookies_array.push(cookie.split('; ')[0])
  }
  cookies = cookies_array.join('; ')

  # following redirect
  response = http.get(response.header['location'], { 'Cookie' => cookies })
  # verify only one item in cart
  expect(response.body).to include("<span id='cart_item_count'>1</span>")
end

response = http.get(buy_testwise_path, { 'Cookie' => cookies })

response = http.get(cart_path, { 'Cookie' => cookies })
expect(response.body).to include("<span id='cart_item_count'>2</span>")
File.open("c:/temp/cart.html", "w").write(response.body)
```

10. Synergy of API and Functional Testing

Modern software usually offer both Web App and Mobile App, as well as API services for integration. From testing's perspective, we can take advantage of the synergy of functional and API testing for a faster and flexible test solution.

In this chapter, I will illustrate with one of most common test case: user registration with email confirmation. While this test case is common, it is often classified for manual testing due to the following challenges for test automation:

- Lack of experience or skills on checking emails with automation scripts
- Prone to SMTP server's unavailability
- Email delivery time is not guaranteed
- Possibility of sending test emails to a real user's email account

Here I will show an easy and reliable testing solution: MailCatcher.

Check emails with MailCatcher

MailCatcher[1], is a "simple SMTP server which catches any message sent to it to display in a web interface". Basically, you configure the test app server to send emails to MailCatcher, MailCatcher displays the received emails in a web interface.

MailCatcher is simple, fast and reliable. It provides a nice interface for visual inspecting emails. More importantly, it is test automation scripts friendly.

Install and start MailCatcher

MailCatcher is developed in Ruby. To install MailCatcher, make sure you have Ruby installed first. Installation is simple, standard gem install from a command line (or Terminal on Linux/Mac) window.

---

[1]http://mailcatcher.me

```
gem install mailcatcher
```

Start the MailCatcher server.

```
$ mailcatcher
Starting MailCatcher
==> smtp://127.0.0.1:1025
==> http://127.0.0.1:1080
*** MailCatcher runs as a daemon by default. Go to the web interface to quit.
```

Open http://127.0.0.1:1080 in browser to verify it is running.

Configure your App to use MailCatcher

Once MailCatcher is up running, you can configure the test server to use it as the SMTP server. Here is a configuration example for Ruby on Rails apps (*config/environments/test.rb*).

```
config.action_mailer.delivery_method = :smtp
config.action_mailer.smtp_settings = { :address => "127.0.0.1", :port => 102\
5 }
```

MailCatcher web site has more examples for other type applications. Besides Ruby on Rails, I have used MailCatcher a number of times for both Java and .NET applications.

 ## Start MailCatcher binding specific IP and port numbers

If you have difficulty accessing the MailCatcher server from other machines, you can start the server by specifying the binding IP address and ports.

```
mailcatcher --ip 10.0.0.15 --smtp-port 25 --http-port 80
```

Example: Test user sign up with email activation link

User registration is probably one of the most common features of a web application. After signing up, the user is usually required to click the activation link in the email sent by the system for verification.

Here is how I test it with SiteWise (one of my web app) using MailCatcher.

Prerequisite:

- MailCatcher is up running (on 10.0.0.15)
- the test server is configured to use MailCatcher SMTP to send emails

High level test steps:

1. Visit MailCatcher Web Interface and clear the emails (to avoid confusion)
2. Drive browser to register a new user
3. Visit MailCatcher Web Interface to open the first email with expected subject
4. Extract out the activation url from the email body
5. Visit the activation url in browser (using Selenium WebDriver)
6. Verify that the user can log in

Verify manually

Here is a screenshot of MailCatcher web interface after receiving the activation email.

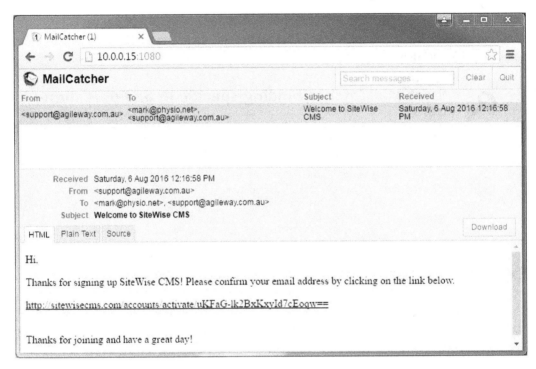

Test script

sign_up_spec.rb

```ruby
# I put mailcatcher functions into a seperate helper file, see below
require File.dirname(__FILE__) + "/../mail_catcher_helper.rb"
require 'faker'

describe "User can Sign up demo.sitewisecms.com" do
  include MailCatcherHelper

  before(:all) do
    @driver = Selenium::WebDriver.for(:chrome)
  end
```

```ruby
after(:all) do
  driver.quit unless debugging?
end

it "Sign up the verify the email" do
  driver.get("http://107.170.251.122:1080")
  sleep 1
  mailcatcher_clear

  driver.get("http://demo.sitewisecms.com/register")
  sign_up_page = SignUpPage.new(driver)
  email = Faker::Internet.email
  sign_up_page.enter_email(email)
  sign_up_page.enter_password("test")
  sign_up_page.enter_password_confirmation("test")
  driver.find_element(:id, "authcode").send_keys("WISE") # raw selenium
  sign_up_page.check_accept_terms
  sign_up_page.click_register

  driver.get("http://107.170.251.122:1080")
  mailcatcher_search("Welcome to SiteWise CMS")
  mailcatcher_open_message_from_top
  # the_email_text = mailcatcher_message_text

  driver.switch_to.frame(0)
  sleep 1  # wait 1 second for email, MailCatcher is fast
  activate_token = ""
  begin
    activate_token = driver.find_element(:id, "activate_link")["data-path"]
  ensure
    driver.switch_to.default_content
  end
  puts activate_token

  driver.get("http://demo.sitewisecms.com" + activate_token)
  expect(page_text).to include("The account is activated successfully")
```

```
driver.get("http://demo.sitewisecms.com/login")
customer_login_page = CustomerLoginPage.new(driver)
driver.find_element(:name, "email").send_keys(email)
driver.find_element(:name, "password").send_keys("test")
driver.find_element(:id, "sign_in_btn").click

driver.find_element(:id, "logout_link").click  # verify it is in
  end

end
```

Some notes.

- The functions starting mailcatcher_ are defined in *mail_catcher_helper.rb*
- I used page objects such as sign_up_page.enter_email("mark@physio.net") wrapped the raw Selenium WebDriver test statements for clarity and maintenance.
- I use Faker::Internet.email to generate different email for each run so that this test can be run many times without getting "the email already exists" errors.
- When an email is opened, it is shown in a bottom frame. That's why I used driver.switch_-to.frame().
- I use begin ... ensure to make sure the Selenium WebDriver is back to the main window even when failed to extract the activation link

The below is a helper (*mail_catcher_helper.rb*) that you might include when using Mail-Catcher.

```
module MailCatcherHelper

  def mailcatcher_clear()
    driver.find_element(:link_text, "Clear").click
    sleep 1
    a = browser.driver.switch_to.alert
    a.accept
  end

  def mailcatcher_open_message_from_top(idx = 0)
    message_rows = driver.find_elements(:xpath, "//nav[@id='messages']/table\
```

```
/tbody/tr")
    message_rows[idx].click
  end

  def mailcatcher_open_message(idx = 1)
    driver.find_element(:xpath, "//tr[@data-message-id='#{idx}']").click
    sleep 1
  end

  def mailcatcher_message_from
    driver.find_element(:xpath, "//dl[@class='metadata']/dd[@class='from']")\
.text
  end

  def mailcatcher_message_to
    driver.find_element(:xpath, "//dl[@class='metadata']/dd[@class='to']").t\
ext
  end

  def mailcatcher_message_subject
    driver.find_element(:xpath, "//dl[@class='metadata']/dd[@class='subject'\
]").text
  end

  def mailcatcher_message_text
    sleep 0.5
    driver.switch_to.frame(0)
    message_body = ""
    begin
      message_body = driver.find_element(:tag_name, "body").text
    ensure
      driver.switch_to.default_content
      return message_body
    end
  end

  def mailcatcher_search(q)
    search_elem = driver.find_element(:name, "search")
```

```
    search_elem.send_keys(q)
    search_elem.clear
    search_elem.send_keys(:tab)
  end

end
```

11. Test Execution

Test automation is much more than writing automated tests. After writing a new test (and it ran fine), I usually spend far more time on test execution to make sure

- the new test runs fine many times
- the new test won't cause other tests to fail

This is to achieve the ultimate goal: all tests run fine. 'Fine' is not the same as 'Pass', it means that the tests accurately reflect the status of application's functionalities. In this chapter, I will show different ways to manage test execution.

Execute RSpec tests from command line

To run test cases in a RSpec test script file:

```
rspec soap_spec.rb
```

Run multiple test script files in one go:

```
rspec soap_spec.rb  rest_spec.rb
```

Run an individual test case in a test script file, supply a line number in a chosen test case range.

```
rspec soap_spec.rb:30
```

To generate a test report (HTML) after test execution:

```
rspec -fh payment_api_spec.rb > test_report.html
```

Here is a sample report:

Execute MiniTest tests from command line

MiniTest[1] is the default testing library for Ruby 1.9.3 and up. MiniTest supports two syntaxes:

---

[1]https://github.com/seattlerb/minitest

- **Test::Unit compatible syntax like xUnit**

  Example (file: *soap_test.rb*):

```ruby
require 'minitest/autorun'

class TestSoap < Minitest::Test

  def setup
    # run before each test case
  end

  def test_soap_with_dynamic_request_data
    file = File.expand_path("../../testdata/c_to_f.xml.erb", __FILE__)
    template_str = File.read(file)
    @degree = 30
    require 'net/http'
    require 'erb'
    request_xml = ERB.new(template_str).result(binding)
    http = Net::HTTP.new('www.w3schools.com', 80)
    resp, data = http.post("/xml/tempconvert.asmx", request_xml,
      {
        "SOAPAction" => "http://www.w3schools.com/xml/CelsiusToFahrenheit",
        "Content-Type" => "text/xml"
      }
    )
    assert_equal("200", resp.code) # OK
    assert resp.body.include?("<CelsiusToFahrenheitResult>86</Celsius")
  end
end
```

- **Expectation syntax like RSpec**

  Example (file: *soap_spec.rb*):

```ruby
require 'minitest/autorun'

describe "SoapTest" do

  before do
    # run before each test case
  end

  it "SOAP with dynamic request data" do
    file = File.expand_path("../../testdata/c_to_f.xml.erb", __FILE__)
    template_str = File.read(file)
    @degree = 30
    require 'net/http'
    require 'erb'
    request_xml = ERB.new(template_str).result(binding)
    http = Net::HTTP.new('www.w3schools.com', 80)
    resp, data = http.post("/xml/tempconvert.asmx", request_xml,
      {
        "SOAPAction" => "http://www.w3schools.com/xml/CelsiusToFahrenheit",
        "Content-Type" => "text/xml"
      }
    )
    resp.code.must_equal("200")
    resp.body.must_include("<CelsiusToFahrenheitResult>86</Celsius")
  end

end
```

To run test scripts in MiniTest, regardless which style you choose, just run as regular ruby scripts.

```
ruby soap_test.rb
```

or

```
ruby soap_spec.rb
```

Sample output:

```
Run options: --seed 37493

# Running:


.


Finished in 0.328762s, 3.0417 runs/s, 9.1251 assertions/s.

1 runs, 3 assertions, 0 failures, 0 errors, 0 skips
```

But you cannot run multiple test script files this way. To do that, we need to use Rake, as shown in next recipe.

Custom MiniTest test execution with Rake

Rake[2] is the de-facto build tool for Ruby. If you are familiar with Java, it is like Ant, but easier. Rake is pre-bundled with the Ruby distribution.

The definitions below (in *Rakefile*) defines a task `wstest_minitest` to run all test under `minitest` folder.

```
require 'rake/testtask'

Rake::TestTask.new("wstest_minitest") do |t|
  t.test_files = FileList["#{$test_dir}/minitest/soap*.rb"]
  t.verbose = true
end
```

To run it

```
rake wstest_minitest
```

If the *Rakefile* is not in the current directory, use `-f` switch to specify:

---

[2]https://github.com/ruby/rake

```
cd ..
rake -f recipes/Rakefile wstest_minitest
```

Custom RSpec test execution with Rake

This is my preferred way to run RSpec tests.

Run selected tests

The Rake task *test:selected* below will run the test cases from two test script files: *ch02_soap_-spec.rb* and *ch03_rest_spec.rb*:

```
gem 'rspec'
require 'rspec/core/rake_task'


# ...


desc "selected key tests"
RSpec::Core::RakeTask.new("test:selected") do |t|
  # list test script files you want to run below
  t.pattern = ["spec/ch02_soap_spec.rb","spec/ch03_rest_spec.rb"]
end
```

Invoke the Rake task (in a command prompt for Windows users) by typing:

rake test:selected

The below is a sample output of executing 14 test cases in those 2 test script files. In this instance, 13 tests passed ('.' means pass, 'F' means failed):

```
....F.........
```

```
Failures:

  1) SOAP Testing SAXON
     Failure/Error: expect(station_name).to eq("Pereire")

       expected: "Pereire"
            got: "Reaumur-Sebastopol"

       (compared using ==)
     # ./spec/ch02_soap_spec.rb:134:in `block (2 levels) in <top (required)>'

Finished in 14.55 seconds (files took 0.59392 seconds to load)
14 examples, 1 failure
```

Run all tests

Quite often you want to run all tests together (as in regression testing), including new ones that might have been added by your colleagues. Here is a Rake task definition to run all test script files ending with _spec.rb in the sub folder spec.

```
desc "Run all RSpec tests in the current folder"
RSpec::Core::RakeTask.new("test:all") do |t|
  t.pattern = ["spec/*_spec.rb"]
end
```

With one line of commands(rake test:all), you can now effortlessly execute a series of tests. However, quite often, we need to exclude some specifics files. This can be achieved by adding an exclusion list as below:

```
# List tests you want to exclude
def excluded_spec_files
  ["spec/ignore_spec.rb", "spec/ch05_email_spec.rb"]
end


desc "Run all RSpec tests in the current folder"
RSpec::Core::RakeTask.new("test:all") do |t|
  all_specs = Dir.glob("spec/*_spec.rb")
  specs_to_be_executed = all_specs - excluded_spec_files
  t.pattern = FileList[specs_to_be_executed]
end
```

Run as part of Continuous Testing

Running tests in CI process, in essence, is invoking build tasks (such as Rake) to run automated test scripts in a CI Server. It makes managing test execution easier, plus other benefits (show later).

Let me show you how to get it done first. I will illustrate with BuildWise, a free and open source CI server for functional testing created by me.

Prerequisite:

- BuildWise Server[3]

  The BuildWise server can be downloaded at the book site[4]. For BuildWise installation, refer the screencasts[5].
- Sample test project: https://github.com/testwisely/test-recipes[6]

  ```
  > cd c:\work
  > git clone https://github.com/testwisely/test-recipes
  ```

1. **Create a new project in BuildWise**

   Click 'New project' and fill two fields: *Name* and *Working folder.*

---

[3]http://testwisely.com/buildwise
[4]http://zhimin.com/books/api-testing-recipes-in-ruby
[5]http://testwisely.com/buildwise/screencasts
[6]https://github.com/testwisely/test-recipes

← → C 🗋 127.0.0.1:3618/projects/new

*build*wise

New project

Option 1. Loading from a working folder or Specify manually

Name:

> API Testing Recipes

Identifier:

> api-testing-recipes

(lower case and unique, e.g. adminwise-ui-tests)

Working folder:

> C:\work\test-recipes

(Specify the SCM checked out project folder on the machine running BuildWise se

SCM Login:

> username   password

(You may want to use dedicated user for CI, if you have set up SSH without login o

Project Template:

> Continuous Test Server   ▾

UI test folder:

*(where the UI tests are, relative to project root directory, eg. **spec** or **ui-tests/spec**,*

Rake Task for UI Tests:

*(e.g. **ci:ui_tests:full**. You may configure this later.)*

> Create   Cancel

Click 'Create' button.

API Testing Recipes 📈
NEVER BUILT

Build Now

2. **Configure the build project**

Click "API Testing Recipes" link on the dashboard to configure.

• Enable and set API Test Task (a Rake task in Rakefile)

Deploy ☐

API Test ☑   -f api-tests/Rakefile ci:test:all

UI Test ☐

The ci:test:all task defined in *Rakefile* as below:

```ruby
# ci_reporter gem runs tests and output in JUnit test report format
gem 'ci_reporter'
require 'ci/reporter/rake/rspec' # use this if you're using RSpec


# ...


# For BuildWise CI
BUILDWISE_URL = ENV["BUILDWISE_MASTER"] || "http://buildwise.macmini"
# the buildwise.rake define tasks to communicate with BuildWise Server
import File.join(File.dirname(__FILE__), "buildwise.rake")


# ...


desc "run all tests from BuildWise"
task "ci:test:all" => ["ci:setup:rspec"] do
  build_id = buildwise_start_build(:project_name => "api-testing-recipes\
",
    :working_dir => File.expand_path(File.dirname(__FILE__)),
    :excluded => excluded_spec_files
  )
  begin
# the results (JUnit style format) saved in spec/reports folder
    FileUtils.rm_rf("spec/reports") if File.exists?("spec/reports")
    Rake::Task["test:all"].invoke
  ensure
```

```
    puts "Finished: Notify build status"
    sleep 2 # wait a couple of seconds to finish writing last test resul\
ts xml file out
    buildwise_finish_build(build_id)
  end
end
```

See above recipes for Rake task: test:all
- Specify the test folders

UI tests (functional tests via GUI)

UI Test folder:	api-tests/spec
	The folder (relative path) contains the mair
Test results folder:	relative path, e.g. spec/reports
	The directory (relative path) contains gene
	spec/reports or log . The output of test
Local working test folder:	C:\work\test-recipes\spec

Save the project.

3. **Click "Build Now" button on Dashboard page**

 API Testing Recipes ⬈
2016-08-28 14:15:43 1 :building   Cancel this build   Now building:

4. **View build**

Click the build (8fd6225b.1 :OK for this example) to view the build details.

API Testing Recipes   Build #1 OK

Started at: 2016-08-28 14:15
Finished at: 2016-08-28 14:15
Duration: 13 seconds

▽ Build artifacts
    📄 build-output.log 0KB
    📄 builder.log 0KB
    📄 changeset.log 1KB

▷ Change log

▽ UI Test Results (6 test cases) | Export Excel , CSV

TEST FILE (6 test cases in 3 test scripts files)	TIME (S)	RESULTS ^
parse_response_spec.rb	0.0	
- Parse XML Parse XML with REXML	0.0	OK
- Parse XML Parse XML with Nokogiri	0.0	OK
restful_spec.rb	2.0	
- REST WebService REST - List all records	1.3	OK
- REST WebService REST - Get a record	0.7	OK
soap_spec.rb	0.6	
- SOAP Testing SOAP with sample XML	0.3	OK
- SOAP Testing SOAP with dynamic request data	0.3	OK

Navigate back to the dashboard, you will see a green lava lamp for the project.

 API Testing Recipes 📈
2016-08-28 14:15:43 8fd6225b.1 :OK (13.0)

Build Now

What are the benfits for doing this way?

- Easy to run all tests

  Just click 'Build Now" button to trigger a build, and project members can view all build

history easily in browser.
- View history of individual test script

restful_spec.rb

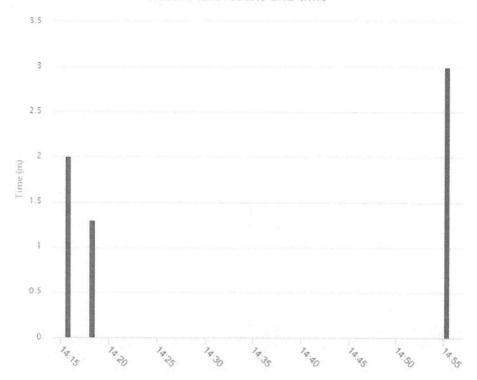

This can help identify regression errors quickly.
- View test script

restful_spec.rb

```
 1  load File.dirname(__FILE__) + '/../test_helper.rb'
 2
 3  require 'net/http'
 4  require 'httpclient'
 5  require 'rexml/document'
 6
 7  describe "REST WebService" do
 8    include TestHelper
 9
10    it "REST - List all records" do
11      list_rest_url = "http://www.thomas-bayer.com/sqlrest/CUSTOMER"
12      resp = HTTPClient.new.get(list_rest_url)
13      xml_doc  = REXML::Document.new(resp.body)
14      expect(xml_doc.root.elements.size).to be > 10
15    end
16
17    it "REST - Get a record" do
18      get_rest_url = "http://www.thomas-bayer.com/sqlrest/CUSTOMER/4"
19      resp = HTTPClient.new.get(get_rest_url)
20      expect(resp.body).to include("<CITY>Brisbane</CITY>")
21    end
22
23  end
```

- Quickly find out which test step failed

```
+    <CITY>Dallas</CITY>
+</CUSTOMER>
./api-tests/spec/restful_spec.rb:20:in 'block (2 levels) in <top (required)>'
```

For this failure, it failed on line 20 of restful_spec.rb.

BuildWise also supports distributing tests to multiple build agents to run them in parallel, which greatly reduces the overall test execution time. Furthermore, BuildWise executes tests in an intelligent order - running most recent failed tests first, which shortens the feedback. I will cover more on test execution in CI in my upcoming book: Continuous Web App Testing[7].

The practices of I used in BuildWise are general, may be applicable to other CI servers.

---

[7]https://leanpub.com/continuous-web-app-testing

Afterword

First of all, if you haven't downloaded the recipe test scripts from the book site[8], I strongly recommend you to do so. It is free for readers who have purchased the ebook through Leanpub.

Practice makes perfect

Like any other skills, you will get better at it by practising more. This is especially true for test automation. Efficient API testing, in my opinion, relies on

- Knowledge of API, such as XPath knowledge for XML
- Scripting/programming skills.
- Understanding of automation, e.g., tests shall be independent from each other.

I have been programming/testing in Ruby for over 10 years. I can still find found a better way to accomplish tasks in Ruby from time to time. It feels good when that happens.

Learn and grow

- **Improve programming skills**

  It requires programming skills to effectively develop API tests in Ruby. For readers with no programming background, the good news is that the programming knowledge required for writing test scripts is much less comparing to coding applications, as you have seen in this book. If you like to learn with hands-on practices, check out Learn Ruby Programming by Examples[9].

- **Learn Functional UI Testing with Selenium WebDriver**

  If you haven't used Selenium WebDriver to write automated test scripts for UI testing, I strongly recommend you to do so. Selenium WebDriver is in big demand, having it on you Resume will help your career. Moreover, I trust the UI scripting ability will benefit your API testing. If you like this book, you may find my other books on UI testing helpful:

---

[8]http://zhimin.com/books/api-testing-recipes-in-ruby
[9]https://leanpub.com/learn-ruby-programming-by-examples-en

     – Practical Web Test Automation[10]
     – Selenium WebDriver Recipes in Ruby[11]

- **Running tests in Continous Testing server**

  Develop the habit to run all tests at least twice a day. To achieve that, you need to run them in a CI server. It will make test execution and detecting regression issues so much easier and quicker. Setting up executing automated tests in CI does require more knowledge, it is not that difficult when you are working with the right kind of CI server, such as BuildWise I showed in Chapter 11.

Best wishes for your test automation!

---

[10]https://leanpub.com/practical-web-test-automation
[11]https://leanpub.com/selenium-recipes-in-ruby

Resources

Books

- **Practical Web Test Automation**[12] by Zhimin Zhan

  Practical Web Test Automation is a guide for you to achieve success in automating testing web applications. Topics include:
  - Developing easy to read and maintain Watir/Selenium tests using next-generation functional testing tool
  - Page object model
  - Functional Testing Refactorings
  - Cross-browser testing against IE, Firefox and Chrome
  - Setting up continuous testing server to manage execution of a large number of automated UI tests
  - Requirement traceability matrix
  - Strategies on team collaboration and test automation adoption in projects and organizations
- **Selenium WebDriver Recipes in Ruby**[13] by Zhimin Zhan

  The problem solving guide to testing web applications with Selenium WebDriver.
- **Learn Ruby Programming by Examples**[14] by Zhimin Zhan and Courtney Zhan

  Master Ruby programming to empower you to write test scripts.

Tools

- **SoapUI**[15]

  A popular tool for testing SOAP Web services, however I only use it to generate sample request XML from WSDL.

---

[12]https://leanpub.com/practical-web-test-automation

[13]https://leanpub.com/selenium-recipes-in-ruby

[14]https://leanpub.com/learn-ruby-programming-by-examples-en

[15]https://www.soapui.org

- **Postman**[16]

  A free Chrome plugin for testing HTTP requests.

---

[16]http://www.getpostman.com